AFRICAN AMERICAN ADOLESCENT FEMALE HEROES

Children's Literature Association Series

AFRICAN AMERICAN ADOLESCENT FEMALE HEROES

The Twenty-First-Century Young Adult Neo-Slave Narrative

Melanie A. Marotta

University Press of Mississippi / Jackson

The University Press of Mississippi is the scholarly publishing agency of the Mississippi Institutions of Higher Learning: Alcorn State University, Delta State University, Jackson State University, Mississippi State University, Mississippi University for Women, Mississippi Valley State University, University of Mississippi, and University of Southern Mississippi.

www.upress.state.ms.us

The University Press of Mississippi is a member of the Association of University Presses.

Copyright © 2023 by University Press of Mississippi
All rights reserved

First printing 2023
∞

Library of Congress Cataloging-in-Publication Data

Names: Marotta, Melanie A., author.
Title: African American adolescent female heroes : the twenty-first-century young adult neo-slave narrative / Melanie A. Marotta.
Other titles: Children's Literature Association series.
Description: Jackson : University Press of Mississippi, 2023. | Series: Children's literature association series | Includes bibliographical references and index.
Identifiers: LCCN 2022053774 | ISBN 9781496844972 (hardback) | ISBN 9781496844989 (trade paperback) | ISBN 9781496844996 (epub) | ISBN 9781496845009 (epub) | ISBN 9781496845016 (pdf) | ISBN 9781496845023 (pdf)
Subjects: LCSH: Slavery in literature. | Young adult literature, American. | African American women in literature. | African American women heroes. | African American young adults—Books and reading. | Afrofuturism. | Science fiction, American—History and criticism. | Speculative fiction, American—History and criticism.
Classification: LCC PS374.S58 M37 2023 | DDC 813/.609352208996073—dc23/eng/20230206
LC record available at https://lccn.loc.gov/2022053774

British Library Cataloging-in-Publication Data available

CONTENTS

Acknowledgments and Dedication. vii

Introduction: Visibility and Inclusivity ix

Chapter 1. Sherri L. Smith's *Orleans* and Karen Sandler's *Tankborn*: The Female Leader, the Neo-Slave Narrative, and Twenty-First-Century Young Adult Afrofuturism 3

Chapter 2. The Safety of Space in Nnedi Okorafor's *The Book of Phoenix* and *Binti* 27

Chapter 3. Afrohorror and the Gendered Narrator: Progression and Regression of the Adolescent Female Activist Character in the Devil's Wake Series and the Parables Series 54

Chapter 4. The Biracial Female Protagonist, Trauma, and Memory in A. J. Hartley's *Steeplejack* 85

Chapter 5. Self-Image and Narration in the Young Adult Steampunk Novels *The Black God's Drums* and the Dread Nation Series 103

Notes 129

Works Cited 133

Index 141

ACKNOWLEDGMENTS AND DEDICATION

I dedicate this book to my mother, who has always stood by me and encouraged me.

I offer my gratitude to Katie Keene, my editor at the University Press of Mississippi, and to the team at the press. My thanks to Dr. L. Adam Mekler at Morgan State University for his continued support. To Dr. Ruthe T. Sheffey for imparting her knowledge of African American women's literature.

INTRODUCTION

VISIBILITY AND INCLUSIVITY

In 2018, Afrofuturism came to the forefront of mainstream popular culture with the release of Marvel's *Black Panther* film.[1] The film industry continues to be extensively criticized for its lack of Black actors and characters, for its too few films including issues pertaining to Black American audiences. In its publication the *Hollywood Diversity Report*, UCLA has documented that there has been an increase in Black actors in film, albeit a small one in 2020 and a more notable one in 2021.[2] The improvement in casting has been recent: the 2021 report identifies what is termed "proportionate representation," meaning that there have been increases for people of color and women in lead actor casting and casting overall (5). It is troubling, however, that, as UCLA shows, although on television there has been a marked improvement in diversity over time, women and people of color have been marginally represented in casting until recently.[3] It is also troubling that women have been continuously vying for a prominent place in film but do not appear to be obtaining one behind the scenes.[4] By March 2022, three women had won the Oscar for Best Director,[5] and only seven had been nominated. None of these directors are Black women.[6] With the 2017 release of *Wonder Woman* (as with *Black Panther*), moviegoers were exposed to a strong lead (and a female director, Patty Jenkins) that defies Hollywood's construct of what a popular protagonist and film entails.[7] It took two films, both falling into the science fiction genre and featuring superheroes (Marvel/Disney and DC Comics) and both popular culture areas with a diehard fanbase for films with female leads, female directors, and Black people for Hollywood to pay attention to what viewers want—and need.

My reasoning behind offering this cinematic commentary at the start of a book about young adult (YA) literature is that the fields of young adult science fiction and speculative fiction face many similar challenges as the film industry. As someone who examines African American women's writings and science fiction, I was noticeably concerned when it came to my attention in 2014 while completing research for the book's initial chapter that few science fiction and speculative works feature African American female adolescent protagonists and the number of additions to these subgenres has been barely perceptible since then. As readers, we are aware that, during the twentieth century, while African American male writers' texts received critical attention, African American women's overwhelmingly did not. It was not until the 1970s that they received critical consideration (thanks to Toni Morrison for her editorial role at Random House and for her release of *The Bluest Eye* in 1970, both of which ensured that African American women's writing had the recognition it deserved).[8]

My first chapter, "Sherri L. Smith's *Orleans* and Karen Sandler's *Tankborn*: The Female Leader, the Neo-Slave Narrative, and Twenty-First-Century Young Adult Afrofuturism," started out as a journal article before being revised for publication in this book. Here, I examine Smith's standalone dystopic novel *Orleans*, in which Smith envisions a segregated future for African Americans. Sandler in *Tankborn* (a trilogy) also creates a society where its members are forcibly separated from one another; however, in this case it is discriminatory actions toward the technologically created rather than marginalization solely based on ethnicity. While completing the research for this essay, which I started in 2014, I discovered few contributions to YA Afrofuturism featuring a female protagonist. What I primarily found was a few articles, including readers' blog entries, mainly written by African American mothers that lamented the lack of works in this field. I was and continue to be intrigued as to why there are numerous YA dystopic texts with Caucasian protagonists, mostly male, but very few with African American female characters (major or minor). The YA dystopic novel has been a niche market, one with limited access for people of color; in the second decade of the twenty-first century this fact appears to be changing.

With the release of the third Maze Runner film, David Sims from *The Atlantic* declares, "And yet as the final act succumbed to dull, apocalyptic formula, I saw an entire sub-genre slip away with it: *The Death Cure* is a grim, half-hearted farewell to this wave of young-adult dystopias." Sims is correct in his assertion, as the decline in the cinematic field has been perceptible, but this is not necessarily a desired outcome by the viewing audience. On 10 February 2018, Eli Glasner from the CBC (Canadian Broadcasting Corporation) published an article online in which he discusses Afrofuturism and its reflection in (at the time) upcoming films, namely *Black Panther*, *A Wrinkle in Time*, and *Brown Girl Begins* (2017), two of which are in the children's/YA fields. Caribbean-Canadian Nalo Hopkinson's *Brown Girl in the Ring* (1998), upon which Canadian director Sharon Lewis based her film, is a notable example of young adult Afrofuturism.[9] In order to save Toronto from corruption, Ti-Jeanne must defeat her grandfather, Rudy; as she does so, Ti-Jeanne learns to value her cultural heritage. The development of Hopkinson's novel into a film, albeit in the smaller Canadian market, shows that there is interest in the young adult Afrofuturism and speculative literature fields, so this book is a timely one.

THE PURPOSE OF THE STUDY, THE SLAVE NARRATIVE, AND THE NEO-SLAVE NARRATIVE

This study investigates the application of the neo-slave narrative structure to the twenty-first-century young adult text. Before delving any further into the field of the neo-slave narrative, some elaboration may be in order. The slave narrative was published as an act of abolition during the antebellum period. While there are famed slave narratives that document the European slave trade (*The History of Mary Prince, A West Indian Slave. Written by Herself* [1831] or *The Interesting Narrative of the Life of Olaudah Equiano, or Gustavus Vassa, the African. Written by Himself* [1789]), it is the textual descendants of the American slave narrative that will be the focal point of this investigation. A slave narrative is an autobiographical self-told story, one that centers on the traumatic experiences of a formerly enslaved person. Since many enslaved people were forced to be illiterate, they did not write their stories themselves, instead reciting their account to a White abolitionist for transcription. The purpose of the slave narrative is to illustrate in great, personal detail the trauma and inhuman treatment faced by enslaved people at the hands of the enslaver, to familiarize people in the North—who may be disconnected from the South—with the atrocities that unfolded toward Black people in the antebellum South.[10]

In addition to the narrative, the autobiographical events are framed with letters from White abolitionists attesting to the validity of the enslavement. Kerry Sinanan discusses pro- and antiabolitionist publications, citing that "abolitionist discourse and literature offered representations of slaves and black people, combined with antislavery opinions and views, which became interwoven in the fabric of slave narratives" (61). The slave narrative became more than a purely autobiographical account of a formerly enslaved person's life; it became the vehicle upon which the hopes for slavery's abolition were pinned. The burden of being a figurehead, an activist for a movement that would eventually free people from bondage, must have been immense. It becomes the formerly enslaved person's duty to not only persuade the reader that enslavement must be abolished but also, so that the former may be accomplished, the formerly enslaved person must convince readers of the humanity of the enslaved. The readers must be convinced that the enslaved are human beings, not property. *If* this is accomplished and *if* those in the North can be convinced enslavement needs to end, then the formerly enslaved person still must battle for equality and societal positioning as a free person.

Connecting the slave narrative to the YA neo-slave narrative, like with the formerly enslaved, the responsibility of telling their story falls on the African American female adolescent much like their predecessors have had to do; now though, the placement of power alters. Again, it is critical to the comprehension of the slave narrative, the neo-slave narrative, and this study that the reader be cognizant of the fact that for Black American women, experiences in enslavement drastically differ from those by men. Elaborating on varied states of imprisonment for Black Americans historically, Patricia Hill Collins writes:

> But just as gender, age, skin color, and class affect the contours of oppression itself, these very same categories shape strategies

of resistance. As African American women's slave narratives point out, men and young people could more easily break out by running away than women, mothers, and older people. Then as now, African American women are often reluctant to leave their families, and many sacrifice their own personal freedom in order to stay behind and care for children and for others who depend on them. (93)

Hill Collins identifies the clear demarcation between the treatment of female and male enslaved people. While completing research for this book, I have encountered a small number of scholars who have attempted to argue the gender fluidity of enslaved women, arguments clearly problematic as gender constructs are societal and during the American antebellum period and Reconstruction overwhelmingly determined by White, male Americans. Enslaved women's lives were distinct because not only were they marked in accordance with sex but by gender construct.[11] Their gender identities were forced on them, determining their place in slaveholding America; in other words, enslaved women, young women, and girls were categorized so that monetary value, societal placement (duties in the slaveholding space), and discriminatory treatment could be assigned.

As Sinanan, Dickson D. Bruce Jr., and I have observed, the slave narrative has been completed as a political tool, one destined to depersonalize the formerly enslaved person, launching them into activist status. For formerly enslaved (freed) and enslaved women especially, the slave narrative continues to be a site of Othering, of marginalization. As formerly enslaved women take control of their stories, White voices (whether at the time of publication or later as theorists) try to dominate by infusing doubt and depersonalization. The Black women of these stories are then reduced to bodies, to degrading stereotypes, to entities with no choices available. Hill Collins's celebration of African American women is key to the formerly enslaved women's actuality. The neo-slave narrative of the twentieth and twenty-first centuries provides a platform for a reclamation of the real and a refutation of the false. Xiomara Santamaria documents an issue inherent to slave narratives written by women, namely the creation of stereotypes regarding their sexuality and their "sexual vulnerability" that were created during the antebellum period (232). Both Hill Collins and Santamaria call attention to the formerly enslaved and enslaved women's reality during the antebellum period, one that reaches well into contemporary analyses of African American female characters as well as actual African American women's and girls' realities. Analyzing the "genderless" construct forced upon enclaved women, Santamaria offers, "De-gendered in the eyes of middle-class readers because they performed field and manual labor (where they were often in the majority), yet also viewed as oversexed because of their sexual vulnerability, slave women faced especially contradictory circumstances when they entered the spheres of antislavery publicity" (232). Here, the physical objectification of the African American woman during the antebellum period and its overreaching effects are visible, that whichever way she turned, she continued to be confined by the system that enslaved her. Readers and writers must be careful to not further victimize formerly enslaved women by casting them into the role of object, as only the body. Further, the notion from Santamaria shows the problematic nature of categorizing enslaved women as genderless: the enslaved person was classified as needed, whether as woman (for purposes mentioned previously) or identity-less property, ergo not a person. So, the question remains: can an enslaved woman be genderless when their lives revolve around their classification as enslaved woman? It remains that gender identity was assigned when needed to enslave women in an oppressive societal space. Some African American free women and women like Sojourner Truth (formerly enslaved) became activists, voices of a generation, were not cast into constructs (Santamaria 234). Santamaria considers Truth's age as a factor in why she was not constructed as a sexual object (235). It is not just formerly enslaved women that obtain their subjectivity in the neo-slave narrative; free women, gay women, women of a certain age,[12] adolescents, and girls are also made visible for readers in this genre: Black womanhood is celebrated, not diminished, in the neo-slave narrative's communal womanhood.

To elaborate, the responsibility of telling the African American woman's story in the neo-slave narrative is in the hands of the writer and the identifying characters. Make no mistake, this is not the disempowering moment that has been well documented on social media during the second wave of Black Lives Matter (2020): these literary contributions are not a means to explain racism to non-Black people. Unlike the slave narrative, where the abolitionists and political motivations attached to abolition influence the formerly enslaved person's narrative, the neo-slave narrative writer has subjectivity, has a voice of their own choosing. Yogita Goyal analyzes the neo-slave narrative, opening the genre up to non-African American contributions. Referencing late twentieth-century contributions to this genre, on the one hand Goyal acknowledges their "ongoing rhetorical and political power," while on the other hand asserts that "much of this literature is in fact animated by a desire to turn to unspeakable figures—whether they are black slave owners, an African father guilty of selling his children, or a fugitive mother who would rather kill her children than have them returned to slavery" (19). While I disagree with much of what Goyal states about the neo-slave narrative,[13] there is value in this idea of the "unspeakable."

In brief, to define a neo-slave narrative a reader must revisit enslavement and the structure of the slave narrative. The goal of the neo-slave narrative is to reclaim the past, one in which Black Americans may have been powerless. I do not wish to assume that all African Americans have the same past experiences during the antebellum period as this is not so; however, there is a complex, shared history for African Americans that the American neo-slave narrative eloquently captures. Goyal alludes to uncovering the past (19–20), that the neo-slave narrative is more than "the recovery of the lost past, or an affirmation of an undifferentiated notion of a black community" (20). Citing Toni Morrison's *Beloved* as the integral illustration of this genre (19), Goyal looks at Margaret Garner's influence on this novel, continuing to affirm that "at the center of many of the most acclaimed of these novels is moral ambiguity, or even the suggestion that no clear ethical choice avails, let alone a redemptive account of history" (20). Morrison's text is important due to her integration of the neo-slave narrative with magical realism[14] and historical fact. Butler's *Kindred* (1979), however, is the ideal example of the neo-slave narrative, the author envisioning how the past affects those in the present, showing the generational scars while doing so. While Goyal sees Garner's reenvisioned story as bringing attention to the "unspeakable," I see the consideration being placed on the agency of the female characters. Neo-slave narratives give African American women a voice in a system where they are continuously faced with racism, misogyny, classism, and age discrimination. The structure and content of neo-slave narratives offer writers a space in which oppressive constructs may not only be challenged but controlled and subsequently obliterated. Many twenty-first-century young adult writers utilizing the neo-slave narrative genre grasp this opportunity to rework the genre, making changes that their readers want to see, namely those that offer inclusion. I posit that the young adult female-led neo-slave narrative can and should show African American young women as the heroes they are in the face of adversity. Successful characters and their creators are activists because they enable young women to see positive, powerful versions of themselves and their ancestors.

The texts I have chosen for this book each feature a female, adolescent protagonist of color. I examine the role of adolescent females of African descent in YA Afrofuturism and YA speculative fiction. As has been oft quoted, Mark Dery offered readers the following delineation of the subgenre: "Speculative fiction that treats African-American themes and addresses African-American concerns in the context of twentieth-century technoculture—and, more generally, African-American signification that appropriates images of technology and a prosthetically enhanced future—might, for want of a better term, be called 'Afrofuturism'" (180). What I wish to report through my research are responses to the following questions. Are the roles for the African American adolescent female character in speculative fiction changing, or are they re-creations of traditional slave narrative roles for females (the enslaved mother figure that creates a community so to save future generations)? Do these writers portray a healing journey for the protagonists? Do they become activists, thereby altering the structure of their societies? When I selected the novels for this study, I endeavored to choose contemporary novels that may reflect issues relevant to adolescents currently. In other words, I wanted to analyze textual contributions that may be relatable to their adolescent audience members. For example, as I discuss in chapter 4, "The Biracial Female Protagonist, Trauma, and Memory in A. J. Hartley's *Steeplejack*," Hartley creates a series in which his female protagonist,

Ang, is biracial and exists virtually unseen on the fringes of society. Ang, who is Lani, is ostracized by both Black and Caucasian societal members; Hartley calls attention to a relatable issue for biracial readers, the feeling as belonging to the in-between space, of not being accepted by either racial group. Rejection due to skin tone (colorism) is not a new subject for exploration in African American literature; however, Hartley ventures into territory not often explored by writers, specifically how adolescents react to this rejection.

Unlike the American slave narrative, which primarily delineates the experiences of enslaved people born into enslavement, the British slave narrative (see Prince and Equiano's works) concentrates on enslaved people who have most likely been taken from their homes and indoctrinated into enslavement. For this book, I have chosen literary contributions from both the United States and Britain as slave narratives tend to primarily originate from formerly enslaved people from these areas.[15] In a fascinating take on the slave narrative, Judie Newman writes, "Drawing on the captivity narrative (though in this case the savage captors are American whites, not Native Americans) and the spiritual conversion narrative (though converting to a belief in freedom and selfhood rather than a Christian God), the slave narratives were published in the nineteenth century to aid the cause of abolition, and enjoyed in massive sales" (26). Slave narratives, as Newman has documented, enjoyed some recognition during the nineteenth century but tended to be for a specialized readership.

Their reincarnation in a newly formed structure, the neo-slave narrative, appeared in the mid-twentieth century and enabled writers to re-create new and symbolic journeys for people of color, those that would resonate with a wider audience due to their inclusion of contemporary issues. In *Race in Science Fiction*, Isiah Lavender posits that a writer "uses technology or science to distance and defamiliarize the institution and practice of slavery, resulting in constructions of slavery as neo-slave narratives or *meta-slave narratives*" (54). Lavender offers that the neo-slave narrative coupled with technology places American enslavement in the background of Afrofuturism. By doing so, Afrofuturism foregrounds the successes of African Americans against the background of enslavement. Many writers, including those associated with the *New York Times 1619 Project*,[16] would deem this an impossibility, stating that American enslavement is aways upfront for African American people. For example, Tracy Deonn's exceptional YA speculative fiction novel *Legendborn* (2020; The Legendborn Cycle), is a twenty-first-century YA neo-slave narrative fantasy set at the University of North Carolina at Chapel-Hill, Deonn's alma mater. Straying for a moment from Afrofuturism as this genre is an offshoot of science fiction therefore concerning technology and the future, Deonn adapts the King Arthur story with a sixteen-year-old African American young woman at the helm. Transitioning away from England to the contemporary American South for this fantasy novel, Deonn impressively weaves a neo-slave narrative, giving Bree Matthews the power that the American enslaved people did not have.[17] Offering insight into the creation of Gilda, the African American lesbian vampire lead of her neo-slave narrative, *The Gilda Stories*, Jewelle Gomez elaborates: "In Gilda, I created a character who escapes from her deep sense of helplessness as a slave and gains the ultimate power over life and death" (Gomez, "Foreword"). This author's new envisioning of the neo-slave narrative, the vampire, and Sheridan Le Fanu's *Carmilla* (1872) encapsulates the vision that some YA writers have for their neo-slave narrative, namely, to rewrite history as one that gives enslaved woman agency she historically would not have had.

• • •

The YA neo-slave narrative text is an opportunity for contemporary writers to not only introduce this genre to a new generation of readers but also continue Gomez's foray into recasting a genre for a generation that desires and needs representation in literary contributions.

The question remains: why is the neo-slave narrative and young adult literature significant? Why has there been a YA speculative fiction boom in the second and third decades of the twenty-first century? More importantly, will this move toward more include YA literature remain? Or is this success brief, connected to the moment? It is no coincidence that there has been a significant rise in publications in YA African American speculative fiction and fantasy.[18] This publishing increase may be linked to the racism associated with and spread by the forty-fifth president of the United States and to the second wave of Black Lives Matter.[19] While not all publications during this period may be deemed YA neo-slave narratives, the evidence of the desire for additions reflecting inclusivity in books is compelling.

Linda Hutcheon identifies social, political, and cultural periods ("timeliness") as an explanation for adaptations, citing this as a reason for adaptations featuring racial issues (143). While Hutcheon does not exclusively concentrate on adaptations about/from African American people in her chapter "Where? When?" her observations are compatible with this examination and my reasoning for an exploration of Frederick Douglass's narrative. In the twenty-first century, some of the more recent adaptations have been those on Broadway, namely *Fences* (with Denzel Washington and Viola Davis), *Hamilton* (Lin-Manuel Miranda), and *Ain't Too Proud: The Life and Times of the Temptations*. Referencing Morrison's *Beloved* and the operatic and cinema adaptations of the novel, Hutcheon identifies that the fame of those associated with productions influence audience perceptions (143). For example, a number of Octavia E. Butler's novels have been optioned and may be produced. In the past, there have been independently produced cinematic adaptations, but unless from a fan base and/or from academics, these films did not receive a great deal of notice. American network FX (owned by Disney) ordered a *Kindred* pilot from Branden Jacobs-Jenkins (writer; *Watchmen* producer), and HBO has ordered a pilot of *Fledgling* with J. J. Abrams et al. as executive producers while Viola Davis's company is at work on an Amazon production of *Wild Seed*, just to name a few (Porter; McConnell). My reasoning for this brief movement into Butler's adaptations is to show that Hutcheon is indeed correct, that the shift and popularity of works are influenced by time, place, and associated fame. As Hutcheon identifies, "An adaptation, like the work it adapts, is always framed in a context—a time and a place, a society and a culture; it does not exist in a vacuum" (142). Here, Hutcheon identifies external forces impacting the adaptation's production. With the rise in African American protest literature (i.e., Angie Thomas's *The Hate U Give*, Nic Stone's *Dear Martin*) that centers on Black children's deaths by the police, the resurgence of the neo-slave narrative and its adaptation for an adolescent readership is logical. The question remains: will the publishing industry change (those that choose to publish and those that choose to write) as a result of African American YA protest literature's inclusion? Or is this a momentary change, those in the industry emphasizing systemic racism because of the desire to conforming to the populist issues and/or is this the commodification of racial issues for gain? Ultimately, it is hoped that the popularity of the neo-slave narrative aids in the visibility of racialized people and the abuses suffered.

WHY REVISIT THE SLAVE NARRATIVE? THE AMERICAN SLAVE NARRATIVE AND FREDERICK DOUGLASS

While Douglass's famed narrative is extensively referenced in this book, though it is male oriented, it has not been done without forethought. Douglass's narrative is the standard for the genre (which its telling in itself) and when reading his work, one cannot doubt the eloquence of his words and the devastation inflicted on not only Douglass but all Black enslaved people in America during the antebellum period. Douglass's narrative becomes the ideal for the genre due to its construction—in particular the portion about the enslaved person's education—and the narrator's gender identity.

The slave narrative as a genre became prominent in America from the 1830s to the end of the Civil War.[20] In Douglass's groundbreaking slave narrative, *The Narrative of the Life of Frederick Douglass, An American Slave* (1845), the author delineates the issues contributing to the marginalization of African Americans in early nineteenth-century Maryland, a state in the slaveholding American South. Douglass's first of three autobiographical accounts was an immensely popular abolitionist work, selling over thirty thousand copies upon its release. In a text that has been extensively criticized for being excessively male-centric and omitting the atrocities perpetuated against African American women, Douglass offers his audience a horrific depiction of enslavement in America while simultaneously and surreptitiously reinforcing the truth of the matter for his readers. In an effort that calls attention to the brutalities affecting enslaved persons in the South, Douglass emphasizes the immediate need to abolish enslavement in America. As he does so, Douglass also includes a pivotal argument designed to evoke an empathetic response from his reader. Alluded to but not in such a manner that some abolitionists (or the soon-to-be if Douglass is successful in his endeavors) would be anxious at the thought of having a person of color as an equal, Douglass intimates that in order for an enslaved person to be truly free, enslaved and free African American people must no longer be dehumanized and instead thought of as persons under American law.

In reference to the oppression of African Americans, focusing primarily on approximately 1830 to 1865, Donnarae MacCann writes, "The conviction that so-called Caucasians constituted a superior group did not originate in the 1830s, but it was increasingly systematized to counter the growing attacks of abolitionists" (3). MacCann, who has here elected to examine the heyday of the slave narrative and the period in which Douglass's originates, continues to state that "Ironically, abolitionists seldom opposed the idea of white superiority, even while presenting strong challenges to the proslavery forces in the South" (3). In *White Supremacy in Children's Literature: Characterizations of African Americans, 1830–1900*, MacCann reviews abolitionists publications intended for an audience of children, noting the prevalence of images meant to promote the inferiority of Black people to Caucasian people, forging stereotypes, thereby attempting to ensure from an early age a lack of equality in Americans. Kari J. Winter examines patriarchal guidelines set forth in Gothic novels and slave narratives that concentrate on women in *Subjects of Slavery, Agents of Change: Women and Power in Gothic Novels and Slave Narratives, 1790–1865*. Discussing power and its influence on and imposition of societal structure, Winter writes, "Dominant ideologies or discourses may define a particular group as powerless, but that group will always resist the dominant definitions. As long as she or he is alive, every human being is a source of power, even though that power may be severely restricted" (112). By telling his story to abolitionists and suffragettes in the mid-nineteenth century, Douglass ensures that his voice is dominant, rather than that of the Caucasian abolitionist, or the enslaver. It is his story being told from his perspective, placing the enslaved's experience at the forefront of the text, therefore showing that Douglass has some agency over the reminder of his life, which is to be spent as a freeman. By doing so, Douglass also makes the enslaved's journey personal for the reader: he connects his image to enslavement (in colloquial terms, he puts a face on it), making sure that those in the North who are emotionally detached from the issue can relate to his struggles. In his well-written essay "Politics in the Slave Narrative," Bruce asserts that "With the rise of abolitionism, as slavery's defenders felt increasingly threatened by antislavery efforts, they advanced an argument presenting the institution as a 'positive good' for the nation and for the slaves as well. The slave narratives challenged that argument by providing first-hand testimony contradicting some of its most crucial contentions" (30). Throughout his narrative and his second autobiographical account, *My Bondage and My Freedom* (1855), which elaborates on his experiences recounted in the first, Douglass completes the aforementioned by Bruce, namely he reflects on his inhumane treatment as an enslaved person and offers his readers an insider's account of the realities of American enslavement.

Even though Douglass's narrative is framed by authenticating sources common to slave narratives, he takes control of his story by using it as a persuasive piece with which he asserts his argument for enslaved persons' freedom and humanity. Douglass appeals to the readers' sensibilities by showing that the experiences that African Americans have are similar to those of the readers, namely by highlighting instances in which free will has been employed. Further, Winter explains, "History has shown continually that no amount of physical force or ideological mystification can permanently deprive a human being of his or her will. The power to choose—in fact, the inevitability of choice—is an inalienable part of being human" (112). In order for Douglass's argument to be convincing, an emotional connection must be forged between the African American enslaved and Caucasian readers in the North, otherwise his text will undoubtedly not achieve the desired results. In his excellent and thorough delineation of the slave narrative's components, Bruce contends that by Douglass offering his own account of the events that transpired while he was enslaved (and by extension similar effects may be achieved by other formerly enslaved people recounting their stories), his agency provides his readers with definitive proof of his capabilities (30). In other words, Bruce says by Douglass skillfully reflecting on his experiences as an enslaved person and arguing for enslavement's abolishment, he refutes the proslavery argument regarding the inferiority of people of color. Bruce continues, "The importance for such a demonstration was widely acknowledged. Most of the narratives included introductions and other testimony from established abolitionist leaders—often white, but sometimes African American—stressing their authors' accomplishments and ability" (30). In reference to Bruce's observations, it is telling that readers, even contemporary ones, are more likely to believe Douglass's accounts of his experiences rather than those of Harriet Jacobs. While Douglass eloquently wrote his account of his life, due to her lack of an education Jacobs had difficulty in this area. As a result, her companion, Amy Post, assisted her in creating *Incidents in the Life of a Slave Girl* (1861); another woman, L. Maria Child, edited her work. Because of this and what readers believe is an implausibility of events, the authenticity of Jacobs's account has been doubted. As contemporary readers, we must ask ourselves if this disbelief stems from the gender identity of the teller, especially as Jacobs's account focuses mainly on the threat of sexual violence. In reference to Jacobs's account, Bruce contends that "Slave women, Jacobs and others stressed, were like other American women in valuing chastity; slavery itself made chastity a virtue that could be all too easily violated. And slaveholders violated their slave women with impunity" (32). Jacobs, using her fictive presence Linda Brent, reveals the oppression that female enslaved persons faced under American enslavement's rule. Often religion is twisted by Caucasian proslavery advocates in order to excuse the abuse of power that enslaved people faced; however, formerly enslaved people claim their power by recording this perversion in their narratives. This possession or repossession of agency is one of the driving factors in the re-creation of American enslavement in the neo-slave narrative.

Throughout his narrative, Douglass makes allusions to the Bible, as Christianity was America's dominant religion at the time. In her chapter "The Slave Narrative and the Literature of Abolition," Sinanan examines Douglass's body of work in connection to the British and American abolitionist movements. Discussing abolitionist rhetoric and their mediums, notably Sinanan elaborates about Thomas Pringle, the *Anti-slavery Reporter*'s editor, and his influence on William Lloyd Garrison, *The Liberator*'s editor and a founding member of the American Anti-Slavery Society. It is the latter publication that Douglass subscribes to at the close of his narrative, thereby calling attention to the fact that he feels comfortable enough to reveal his place of residence and is financially stable enough to take on a subscription. Emphasis in Sinanan's chapter, specifically the section regarding Pringle, is on the role of religion, which is so often highlighted in examinations of slave narratives. Referencing Pringle's sonnet "So Help Me God" and Garrison's use of it "to express solidarity" regarding the abolitionist movement, Sinanan writes, "It is important to note the Christian element of this commitment [to the movement] . . . for the renewed activity of the abolitionist movement at this time of American revivalism was intimately connected with an evangelical reconfiguration of slavery as a personal transgression against the will of God" (Sinanan 67). Throughout his narrative, Douglass makes repeated allusions to religion, emphasizing that enslaved African Americans are equal in the eyes of God and, consequently, all members of humanity have free will. He employs Christianity, with which his readers would be able to relate and be properly appalled as they witness the biblical violations that occur in the South.

Early in his narrative, so that he may successfully illustrate the lives of the enslaved for an audience unfamiliar with the atrocities that the enslaved face, one of which is the enslaved's dire need for sustenance, Douglass connects the Genesis myth regarding the Garden of Eden to Colonial Lloyd's garden in Tuckahoe. Here, Douglass recounts instances in which numerous visitors have come to the plantation specially to witness the splendor that is the garden. In her appraisal of Douglass's structure in which Sinanan calls his narrative "the quintessential expression of black freedom" she reports that "its very sophistication and complexity went so far beyond the established conventions of the slave narrative genre that the *Narrative* may be thought to be, '*sui generis*,' as Deborah McDowell observes" (Sinanan 68). By no means may the comparison between Douglass's description of the garden and that in Genesis be deemed accidental. Douglass paints the garden as one that, on the surface, is a utopic space offering visitors a site of seldom before seen splendor. Perceptibly,

Douglass highlights the overflowing sustenance, including apples, and represents the space as a form of temptation for the enslaved and as exclusively for Caucasians. In this instance, Douglass offers a parable to his readers, attempting to show that even though all are created equal in the eyes of God, the enslavers are restricting access to the garden, thereby depriving Black persons of God's favors. Suffering from starvation, some of the enslaved choose to enter the garden and take food undeterred by the threat of punishment if caught. This moment illustrates not only that enslaved people have free will, the ability to choose, but the right to do so as well. In his discussion of late twentieth-century and early twenty-first-century narratives that concentrate on the issue of trauma, Alan Gibbs examines the similarities and differences in structure. Gibbs writes that in the former time frame "traumatic content is paramount and is communicated with a detectable urgency" (46). In the first few chapters sandwiched between autobiographical information is Douglass's commentary regarding enslaved people's lives.

In chapters two through four, Douglass takes an emotional step back, distancing himself from the material and depersonalizing the events. This by no means harms the narrative, but rather allows Douglass to present his readers with a wider frame of reference, to ensure that it is clear how many people have been affected by the institution of slavery. Overall, Douglass's narrative has a tone of "urgency," without directly requesting but insisting that the reader recognize the mortality of the enslaved. In her discussion of free will, Winter reports that "dominant classes have defined women and slave men as intellectually inferior, subhuman creatures who exist as mere extensions of the patriarch's will. However, at the same time, masters have constantly stressed the need for women and enslaved men to obey, which implies that they have a will" (112). By electing to enter the garden seeking food, the enslaved in the narratives have chosen what may be considered the lesser of the two evils: definite suffering due to starvation versus possibly getting caught and subsequently punished. This scene and others like it involving Douglass himself (Douglass refuses to be assaulted on numerous occasions and retaliates rather than submitting to violence) definitively reveals some of the tenets of the slave narrative, religion and free will; however, as this examination is about female characters, a question remains. In Douglass's text, where are the women?

LANGUAGE EMPLOYED IN DISCUSSIONS: THE SLAVE NARRATIVE

Before I continue this examination and delve into Douglass's influence on contemporary neo-slave narratives, the changes in language for the address of slave narratives/neo-slave narratives must be investigated. Eric Zorn (2019) for the Chicago tribune dives into the changes being made to ensure that language is inclusive rather than offensive. While much of the article is not relevant to the issue at hand—and neither women nor misogynistic language is covered in the article— Zorn does call attention to the need for change regarding the address of enslaved people. In "Language Matters: The Shift from 'Slave' to 'Enslaved Person' May Be Difficult, but It's Important," Zorn writes, "A debate has been percolating for the last quarter-century or so—mostly in academia—about whether 'slave' is a needlessly dehumanizing word to describe a person who was in bondage." I have observed the alteration in language, making sure that this book contained the most up-to-date terminology in the analysis of the twenty-first-century neo-slave narrative. It is imperative that the trauma inflicted in the nineteenth century not continue to be perpetuated now, especially in the study of works written for young people, those most susceptible to harm from racist terminology.

In his article, Zorn points to Katy Waldman's *Slate* article (2015) as a precursor to his, both writers indicating Eric Foner as a theorist against the alteration of language regarding enslaved people. According to Foner, he chooses to use the language of Douglass, that to Foner the connotation of slave denotes both personhood and commodity. Waldman disagrees; she states that "sugarcoating the language of historical recall wastes an opportunity to reinforce slavery's inhumanity, to hammer home the brutishness of the perpetrators' worldview by forcing readers to inhabit it." Whatever the theorists' point of view, one glaring fact remains: formerly enslaved persons wrote (or enlisted others) to save the lives of those still enslaved in the

South. The language was not of their choosing but of the abolitionists', some of which may have vied for their freedom but not for their equality. In addition, as academics are aware, we must continuously update our subject area knowledge: this includes language employed in our examinations. It would be unwise to employ dated language, language that may continue to work to oppress the people involved. Conclusively, the language used in examining slave narratives must convey personhood; in other words, while slave denotes a certain space of being, the emphasis is not on the humanity of those oppressed. Enslaved or enslaved person denotes to the reader that the responsibility of the enforced confinement falls on others, that African Americans have had something of violence done to them—there is a definite improvement to the language originating centuries ago.

THE WOMEN IN DOUGLASS'S NARRATIVE AND THEIR EFFECTS ON LATER TEXTS

Following the structure of the slave narrative, Douglass begins his autobiography with information regarding his birth. As this work was published in the mid-nineteenth century, readers would be expecting details to be given about the teller's background in order to determine the plausibility of the events. In the nineteenth century, societal guidelines dictated that one's familial background must be known. Unfortunately, for the formerly enslaved person, this information tended to be unknown; this omission and some members' discriminatory behavior resulted in the doubting of some formerly enslaved people's stories (see, e.g., Jacobs). As we are dealing with the narrative of a formerly enslaved person, Douglass is not himself furnished with a great deal of information about his past, including his birth date. Douglass does, however, to the best of his ability paint his readers a portrait of his mother, Harriet Bailey, and a female enslaved person he refers to as Aunt Hester. As Douglass reports that there are rumors among the enslaved that his enslaver is his father and informs his readers that his mother is enslaved, he also intimates that his father has raped his mother, showing that he is a product of violence. Bruce comments on the slave narratives and women, noting, "The evocation of proslavery hypocrisy was especially striking in regard to sexuality. The portrayal of male slaveholders as sexual predators was common. As the narrators said, slaveholders had the power to compel slave women to submit to sexual advances, and they used it" (32).

I have undertaken extensive research (publications and conference presentations) in the areas of African American literature featuring female characters and science fiction. I have observed that, overwhelmingly, examinations of young adult texts featuring female characters of African descent in science fiction and/or dystopian literature are either (a) negative, or (b) relatively absent. It is my hope that this book will both offer positive portrayals of female characters of African descent and fill a void in this area of research. Douglass shows his readers the lack of power the female enslaved people have over their bodies through the description of the travesties that happened to Aunt Hester and his mother. Jacobs's text is still criticized by readers (including academics) as many doubt that she was capable of hiding in an attic for seven years to avoid being raped by her enslaver.

The female protagonist's agency over her body and her life are issues that I explore throughout the chapters. In chapter 2, "The Safety of Space in Nnedi Okorafor's *The Book of Phoenix* and *Binti*," I examine a selection of Okorafor's novels and novellas, concentrating on how marginalization and overcoming it to assert herself changes her identity. Husband and wife team, Steven Barnes and Tananarive Due, paired to write the new series revolving around female and male adolescent protagonists. In chapter 3, "Afrohorror and the Gendered Narrator: Progression and Regression of the Adolescent Female Activist Character in the Devil's Wake Series and the Parables Series," I delve into Barnes and Due's series (2012, 2013) examining the parallels that appear between their YA texts and Butler's iconic Afrofuturist Parables series. My concerns about Barnes and Due's passive female protagonist are addressed in this chapter. In chapter 5, "Self-Image and Narration in the Young Adult Steampunk Novels *The Black God's Drums* and the Dread Nation Series," I discuss how P. Djèlí Clark and Justina Ireland rewrite the American Civil War, calling attention to discrimination against Black young women and showing readers this momentous event though the eyes of young, Black female characters. In fact, the three prose works selected from these authors are populated primarily with female characters, a welcome change to the genre. The texts from Clark and Ireland are later twenty-first-century additions to the young adult slave narrative genre, and it may be that with the second and third decades of this century, writers are looking toward female inclusivity. As will be observed throughout this monograph, female gender identity, ethnicity, and age must be examined together, as they affect how readers must view the protagonists' experiences and how the aforementioned are portrayed. I have hope for forward-thinking contributions to the young adult female-led neo-slave narrative.

AFRICAN AMERICAN ADOLESCENT
FEMALE HEROES

Chapter 1

SHERRI L. SMITH'S *ORLEANS* AND KAREN SANDLER'S *TANKBORN*

The Female Leader, the Neo-Slave Narrative, and Twenty-First-Century Young Adult Afrofuturism

In an effort to ensure that the past is remembered and the female-centered aspects of the slave narrative are reinforced, the female neo-slave narrative was created (Beaulieu xvi). Elizabeth Ann Beaulieu writes, "Contemporary writers have embraced slavery . . . the details of the enslaved existence become a sort of homage to the very humanity of the protagonists and lends to the works a reverence for the past and its attendant hardships" (xvi). Ashraf Rushdy defines neo-slave narratives as "contemporary novels that assume the form, adopt the conventions, and take on the first-person voice of the antebellum slave narrative" (*Neo-Slave Narratives* 3). Unfortunately, the majority of slave narratives tend to be focused on the male experience rather than that of the female. The neo-slave narrative is a way for contemporary writers to reinforce the African American female experience.

In the young adult Afrofuturistic novel *Orleans* (2013), Sherri L. Smith creates a neo-slave narrative and thereby sends a positive message about the strength of African American females to her readers. Smith's fifteen-year-old female protagonist, Fen de la Guerre, lives in a postapocalyptic urban space. Hurricanes and plague—Delta Fever—decimate New Orleans; as a result, the government has quarantined the city behind a wall. Those that reside in Orleans are carriers of the fever, which is transmitted by blood. In an effort to stop the disease from spreading, the survivors have separated into tribes according to blood type; those with O-type blood are inherently more resistant to the fever. This grouping of individuals is reminiscent of segregation, but, at first, they look as if they have been selected for self-protection rather than forced by racial discrimination.

Elizabeth Anne Leonard states that in science fiction, race tends not to be highlighted but, instead, appears as one of a character's physical attributes (254). Leonard also notes that in some cases, the issue is bypassed entirely (254). Whereas in Smith's text, Fen's race is given a cursory mention, Karen Sandler's *Tankborn* (2011) centers on the issue of race and its influence on identity (Leonard 254). In *Tankborn*, societal prejudice segregates characters, placing them into a caste system. Much like Fen, Sandler's protagonist, Kayla, exists in a society divided into trait-specific groupings. This society, however, is designed to oppress those deemed necessary for physical labor. Kayla's societal placement is determined by her physical appearance and her origins, which categorize her as a GEN (a genetically engineered human). Lokian society, which is based upon the caste system, considers a GEN to be a human engineered in a tank, rather than born from a human female. When Kayla asks her highborn friend, Devak, how society decides hierarchal order, he responds, "You're tankborn. My mother gave birth to me" (Sandler ch. 18). Notably, Kayla and some other GENs have been categorized as such even though their mother gave birth to them, a fact revealed to Kayla later in the novel. The discrimination that both Fen and Kayla experience during their respective quests for freedom is reminiscent of that portrayed by the enslaved in African American narratives. The examination for this study is as follows: in order to ensure the survival of the future generations, Smith's Fen and Sandler's Kayla place themselves figuratively in the role of mother, specifically the twenty-first-century version of the slave narrative mother—the community leader.

The common thread throughout YA dystopian literature featuring female protagonists is the protagonist's journey from object to subject, from powerless to powerful. Sara Day, Miranda Green-Barteet, and Amy Montz assert, "Contemporary dystopian literature with adolescent women protagonists place young women in unfamiliar, often liminal spaces—caught between destructive pasts and unclear futures—in order to explore the possibilities of resistance and rebellion in such unreal settings" (7). Writers focusing their examinations on YA dystopian novels featuring female protagonists often highlight the fluctuating state of the protagonist's identity and lifestyle, arguing that it is symbolic of the transitional position of the adolescent, which also ensures that the audience can relate to the text at hand. Day, Green-Bartleet, and Montz set out the standard formula for the structure of YA dystopian texts in their introduction, as do the contributors in their collection. The issue that should be noted, however, is that in many twenty-first-century dystopian texts featuring female protagonists, writers utilize a White protagonist, thereby relegating characters of color to minor roles. In Smith's *Orleans*, ethnicity is alluded to—Fen is African American—but not explicitly featured. Although the novel does not focus on race, Smith has structured her text to include traditional aspects of the slave narrative, thereby making Fen's bildungsroman journey from oppressive forces to self-actualization take on a new significance.

In many YA dystopian novels, stage one of the protagonist's identity development begins by showing the reader the protagonist's place in society as object. In other words, Fen is not powerless, but her behavior is dominated by the desires of others. In a traditional slave narrative, authenticating accounts from White sources are placed before and after the story of the formerly enslaved person. As Robert B. Stepto observes, "These other voices may belong to various 'characters' in the 'story,' but mainly they appear in the appended documents written by slaveholders and abolitionists alike" (3). In some instances, this type of authentication, that which originates from White sources, serves to place the narrator in a subordinate position. Smith has structured her novel much like a slave narrative, dividing her novel into two sections. Smith has placed a "Before" section from 2014 in advance of Fen's 2056 "After" section, not to validate Fen's story, but rather to show societal aspects from the past that cannot be re-created in Fen's present (Elphick 184). According to Ruth Levitas, "Dystopia (or anti-utopia) represents the fear of what the future may hold if we do not act to avert catastrophe, whereas utopia encapsulates the hope of what might be" (190). In the "Before" section, the narrator does not give information about Fen. Instead, this section functions as a way for the reader to contrast what life is like before and after the onset of the disease and the governmental separation of Orleans from the rest of America. Regarding Octavia E. Butler's dystopic Parables series, Keith Elphick writes, "Unlike many novels in the 'topia' genre, Butler understands that once a society has declined past a certain point of debasement, there is no returning to antiquated notions of the past" (184).

In the "Before" section, which serves as the authenticating section of this neo-slave narrative, the writer has included an except capturing life in New Orleans previous to Hurricane Katrina (the Brossard portion), statistical data regarding the seven hurricanes and their subsequent results, the Declaration of Quarantine, and the Declaration of Separation. This section of the text also serves to show the reader what society was once like and that it may not be re-created. The authors of the historical documents—Quarantine and Separation—are FEMA (US Federal Emergency Management Agency) and government officials including the president of the United States. The official documents are placed in between those that offer a subjective portrayal of pre- and posthurricane New Orleans. They act as a barrier, a symbolic representation of the wall that separates Orleans from the Outer States. Notably, while the purpose of the inclusion of both these sections offers the reader insight into the tremendous alterations made to New Orleans pre-/posthurricane, they also provide insight into the ideology of the space. Rosemarie Garland Thomson examines the American freak show in 1800s America. As she delineates the reasoning behind the existence of the freak show, she also dissects American ideology regarding power, conquest, and normality. Thomson asserts, "The body's material authority provides a seemingly irrefutable foundation upon which the prevailing power relations can thus be erected" (64). Here, the theorist is discussing immigration from Europe, the subsequent colonization of America, and the creation of the American democratic system (64). Thomson continues, "The figure of the freak is consequently the necessary cultural complement to the acquisitive and capable American who claims the normate position of masculine, white, nondisabled, sexually unambiguous, and middle class" (64). Seemingly, in an effort to ease the plague's momentum, the government and FEMA have chosen to quarantine Louisiana and other states with infected inhabitants. By forcefully separating the two spaces, these two groups have identified the Outer States as normative while that behind the wall becomes the unseen spectacle. In order to effectively contrast Orleans and the Outer States, thereby revealing the resilience of the people behind the wall and their oppression by the militarized government, the "Before" authenticating portion needed to be included in Smith's text. It serves to show how Fen and her community are objectified by the political system in the Outer States. Once "After" begins and the alternating narrators are introduced, *Orleans* is shown to be what Stepto terms an "integrated narrative" (5).

The "After" section contains two narrators, Fen and Daniel, a scientist from the Outer States who comes to Orleans to find a cure for the plague. In the integrated slave narrative, the reader is exposed not only to the account of the formerly enslaved person but also to other speakers that relate and authenticate the narrator's account. Stepto relates that it "may be dominated either by its tale or by its authenticating strategies" (4). In this case, Fen takes the position of the "slave" and Daniel, through his narrative, attempts to "dominate" Fen's narrative (4). First, by having "Before" and "After" sections, Smith shows the past utopic space (New Orleans) and present dystopic space. Second, the two sections offer the reader conflicting views of the Orleans body. Thomson describes the gaze of the "idealized American" on the bodies of those contained within the freak show; Thomson states, "The American is mobile, entering and exiting the show at will and ranging around the social order, but the freak is fixed, confined by the material structures and the conventions of the staging and socially immobilized by a deviant body" (65). "Before" features a musician, Edmund Broussard, who is shown only this once in the text. This section provides the reader with a vivid impression of the lifestyles that were irrevocably altered with the segregation of Orleans. Here, the trumpet player Brossard climbs the stairs to the New Orleans landmark Café Du Monde and plays a song famously linked to this space and to Louis Armstrong. Broussard performs "When the Saints Go Marching In," surrounded by others that chose to remain in New Orleans even though the warning regarding Hurricane Ivan had been given. The resilience of the New Orleans people is well known and is portrayed by Smith when the narrator, in reference to Brossard and the city, states, "He was not leaving his home. New Orleans would stand against any storm that came her way" (Smith

"Before"). Smith documents the emotional attachment that the people of New Orleans have for the city and for its lifestyle; the writer also notes that Brossard, representing the majority of the inhabitants of the city, has both freedom of choice and of movement. The narrator observes Broussard's body: "The TV crews love it, the image of a lone man facing nature, refusing to bend" ("Before"). Brossard is New Orleans' "deviant body" because he defies the evacuation order (Thomson 65). The list of hurricanes, the FEMA order, and the declaration from the remainder of America serve to act as the wall has for those with the plague. The people of New Orleans first become the spectacle by the television crews and next by the wall. The American public witnesses Brossard and those that chose to remain—the rebellious masses—from afar. Thomson reveals that "the American is rational and controlled, but the freak is carnal and contingent" (65). Brossard's devotion to the city is passionate and deeply rooted; this attitude may be seen in other characters in the "After" section, but the amount of them is waning. The wall allows for the American ideal to remain on one side of the barrier while the Other exists safely behind it, unrestrained behavior away from those deemed the social norm (Thomson 65).

In "After," Fen's story is juxtaposed with Daniel's, but it is Fen's voice that is first heard from Orleans. Farah Mendlesohn examines the young adult ensemble novel, citing that the appearance of the alternating narrator in the early twenty-first-century series *Remnants*, which was written by K. A. Applegate (Mendlesohn 127). Regarding Applegate's series, Mendlesohn studies both the male and female speakers, observing that this type of rotating narrator offers the reader the opportunity to see through the eyes of both genders. In her intensive study of young adult novels (1999–2007), Melanie D. Koss offers numerous explanations for the rise in young adult texts containing the alternating narrator (Koss). The issue of fragmentation, one that is prevalent in twenty-first-century literature, is discussed by Koss; in one instance Koss attributes the alternating narrators, the fragmented structure, due to the alteration of the transmission of information to adolescents in this century, namely technology. Koss, who also considers alterations that may be made to methods of teaching young adult literature, states that as adolescents' reading methods alter, so must a writer's literary presentation. Like Mendlesohn, Koss examines the attributes of the narrator and his or her relationship with the reader: "Novels written in different voices and with different perspectives can provide teens with ideas of how to act in different circumstances, as well as allow them to experiment with different ideas of identity" (Koss). Koss classifies texts in accordance with both narrative method of transmission and structure of plot. In her study, Smith's novels would be included in the "One Story, Multiple Perspectives" grouping: "Novels that tell one story, but the tale is told via alternating narrators or perspectives" (Koss). As observed earlier, this novel also follows the authenticating slave narrative pattern. This type of narration, that which alternates, serves to temporarily place Fen in a subordinate position.

Daniel's point of view—the voice from the Outer States—for a time appears more valuable than Fen's. Here, the category that Koss calls "Point of View" should be considered: "The alternating either between narrators and/or between first and third person" (Mendlesohn 127). Daniel enters the text, and his motivations appear to be honorable—he desires to cure the plague, thereby offering freedom for generations trapped behind the wall. There is, however, the revelation that his younger brother, Charlie, has died from the fever that is a cause for the reader's concern. As he remembers his brother, he becomes upset and refers to himself as "Danny," clearly his childhood nickname (Smith ch. 5). Daniel's primary drive to find the cure is not humanitarian, but rather guilt. As Daniel's events unfold, the pronounced differences between Fen's and Daniel's accounts become clear. Gender aside, Daniel's account is transmitted using third-person narration, beginning in the Outer States (outside of the wall). While third person offers the reader a more thorough overview of events, it is less personal. Authenticating documents tended to be from those that knew the formerly enslaved person and could attest to the validity of the narrative. While the documents' writers may be familiar with the formerly enslaved person, these documents offer less intimate knowledge of the interworkings of enslavement. By including Daniel's account and doing so through a third-person narrator, Smith allows her reader to place themselves in the text, seeing Fen's society from a distance. He is an outsider attempting to enter what is considered by the Outer

States as an uncivilized space. He symbolically takes the role of the colonizer: he enters Fen's space and attempts to impose his society's rules upon it. As has been previously stated, Daniel momentarily takes control of the narrative, but Fen's voice is ultimately in control of the narrative and of the events that unfold. The predominance of Fen's voice is also meant to show that, like Lauren from Butler's Parables series, Fen's code of conduct, her approach to life, will ensure the survival of future generations (Elphick 185). As Elphick observes, it is not the adults with their past societal notions that will be successful, but the youth of the present with their new outlook on life. Eventually in the novel, Fen's voice will dominate Daniel's, thereby showing that hope for the Orleans' future generations exists with an African American female who prizes community and survival.

In her first stage of development, Fen is subject to the ideologies of adults: her parents, her tribe, and the Outer States' government. As the "After" section, which is aptly titled "Tribe," begins, Fen seems like a typical YA dystopian protagonist. Balaka Basu, Katherine R. Broad, and Carrie Hintz identify the primary themes in YA dystopian literature, noting "conformity" as a method of achieving status as object (3). The authors demonstrate how "often such conformist societies embrace their uniformity out of a fear that diversity breeds conflict" (3). Fen is first shown at the Orleans' market involved in an illegal blood trade with McCallan, a smuggler. Members of her tribe are not permitted to trade for blood because it is dangerous. Fen looks like she is rebelling against her community's precepts by engaging in this trade. She is, in fact, trying to protect Lydia, her tribe's chief, by obtaining untainted blood for her. Lydia is about to give birth, and Fen thinks that she may need a blood transfusion. Lydia is both Fen's community leader and her surrogate mother, so she takes on substantial risks to protect her and the tribe. While Fen appears to be rebelling against her tribe's guidelines by bartering for blood, she is, in fact, offering her subjectivity to the head of her tribe. Even though Orleans does not have an official governing head (Pulliam 172), the behavior of the populace is guided by the chief of each tribe and, through them, the precepts of the government are transferred.

Fen, like Katniss in Suzanne Collins's novel *The Hunger Games*, transcends the constraints of the gender-based roles assigned to her by her society, as evidenced in both her actions and appearance. When Fen initially appears in the novel, her behavior is comparable to that of enslaved persons in narratives instead of a community leader. While a small number of female enslaved people were expected to perform domestic duties, such as working in the houses, the majority worked in the fields completing the same tasks as men. In her discussion of masculine and feminine behavior in District 12 of Suzanne Collins's *The Hunger Games*, June Pulliam relates that "women of the districts do not have the luxury of cultivating learned helplessness or dressing in ways that would constrain their mobility, as their labor is required to ensure the survival of all" (175). *The Hunger Games*, one of the most famed YA dystopian novels in existence, is similar to Smith's novel, as both *Orleans* and *The Hunger Games* are reminiscent of the slave narrative. Fen's and Katniss's actions are similar to that of the female enslaved person, meaning that they are willing to complete any task necessary to ensure the survival of their respective communities (Pulliam 176). In reference to the formation of identity, Roberta Seelinger Trites remarks, "How an adolescent defines herself in terms of race, gender, and class often determines her access to power in her specific situation" (*Disturbing* 47). When Smith introduces Fen, she is trading for untainted blood. Because the marketplace is dangerous, she trades outside of it instead of in it. Fen is not clearly marked as masculine or feminine by her appearance, nor is her ethnicity clearly identified. The only identifier of both gender and ethnicity is a minor note Smith includes about Fen's hair: Lydia, her tribe's chief, has plaited it in braids and piled it on her head. Fen also says that McCallan refers to her during the trade as "Miss Fen" and suggests that she may be the one who is pregnant (Smith ch. 1). Fen's description of her physical appearance and McCallan's statements label her female; her placement and behavior at the market, a traditionally female space, make her gender neutral. Because she takes the role of the caregiver, she is female, even though she may not otherwise appear to belong to this gender. She follows the guidelines of her society by protecting Lydia, the member that can assist in her survival, so Fen's breaking the rules about illegal blood trades is well worth the risk to her. Since *Orleans* is a twenty-first-century YA dystopian novel, Fen, like Katniss, is able to transverse traditional gendered boundaries. In fact, when Fen is labeled feminine rather than gender neutral, she is less powerful, less effective in her tasks. McCallan attempts to take advantage of Fen, retaining the gold she has given him without giving her the blood. When Fen calls attention to McCallan's ogling her and demands her refund, he complies.

In the first stage of her development toward becoming the community leader, Fen is compliant with the guidelines of her society. Repeatedly in the novel, Fen states, "Tribe is life" (Smith ch. 8). The code for survival has been taught to Fen first by her father and then by her chief; these behavioral guidelines are revealed in fragments until the second stage of Fen's development, where more information is disclosed. By herself, Fen ventures away from her tribe in order to procure the supplies needed in order to ensure her leader's survival. Fen rigorously follows social procedures and exudes confidence while away from Lydia. Once her gaze falls upon Lydia, however, Fen reveals her liminality with regard to gendered behavior. Pulliam notes that Collins's Katniss despises her mother's failure to care for her family and sees it as "feminine weakness" (175). In a similar moment, when Fen encounters Lydia tending to the sick in the hospital, she feels uncomfortable and inadequate. Fen describes Lydia's appearance, highlighting distinctly feminine features—braids and a dress. Comparing Lydia's appearance to her own, Fen thinks that Lydia looks "like a queen," whereas she is "a scarecrow next to her" (Smith ch. 1). Fen is highly critical of Lydia's femininity; the comments she makes are a defense mechanism used to mask her true feelings of uncertainty. Lydia is shown as feminine and a leader; Fen calls attention to her sovereignty and her advanced pregnancy. In her statement, Fen refers to herself as unrefined and a follower, not like Lydia. To Fen, Lydia completes the ultimate transgression, placing herself in danger of contracting the plague, but Fen is powerless to stop her. Fen's "access to power" has been negated (Trites *Disturbing*, 47). Even though she is close to Lydia, Fen's self-importance has been deflated. She has been reduced to inexperienced adolescent and community member rather than mature, confident leader.

In the first stage of Fen's development, Lydia is the slave mother figure, but once she dies, Fen takes on this role. In Fen's second stage, she unconsciously takes action in order to alter the future for Lydia's newborn child, aptly named Baby Girl. In reference to the slave mother and her legal state as property, Beaulieu observes that any offspring "would by law follow the condition of their enslaved mother" (18). Just as children of enslaved people become enslaved themselves, children born in Orleans are objectified as their families are before them. They are not valuable Outer States citizens, but remnants of a former society monitored by the Outer States' government. Smith continues to follow the pattern of the slave narrative: the child, Baby Girl (later named Enola), is forcefully separated from her mother, only to be raised by a surrogate parent, Fen. Historically, in the antebellum South, children born into slavery were frequently removed from their mothers at an early age to be raised by elderly female slaves. According to Douglass, this occurred because enslavers desired to stifle or destroy the emotional attachment an enslaved child has to his or her mother. When Lydia dies after giving birth, Fen feels obligated to take responsibility for Lydia's child, as Lydia was her chief and surrogate mother. During Baby Girl's birth, Fen's O-positive (OP) tribe is massacred, so, in actuality, Fen and Baby Girl are the only community each other has remaining. Fen goes to great lengths to save Lydia's child from becoming infected with the fever. At this point in her development, Fen is not emotionally attached to Lydia's child, but she still sees herself as an OP rather than an individual. Beaulieu identifies the neo-slave narrative as concentrating on developing the main character's identity and her connection to her enslaved family (25). Once Lydia dies, Fen draws on the teachings from her past, which help her to form an identity as an individual; her individuality is Fen's third stage of development. As a young child, Fen loses two communities: her parents and that at the research institute. In her youth, Fen and her parents reside at a research institute because the scientists claim that by studying her they can cure the plague.[1] Fen's objectification via Smith's allusion to medical experimentation on African Americans is apparent here. In this second stage, these communities are gone and all that remains is the knowledge that they passed on to her, which often appears in the form of memories. These teachings guide Fen's life choices, and these memories are how she makes contact with her past relations as Beaulieu observes.

By intermixing Fen's memories and her present-day accounts, Smith highlights the influence of her various communities on the formation of her identity. As Fen's tribe lies in ruins, she chooses to hide with Baby Girl but inadvertently falls asleep. When Fen rises, she discovers that she is grasping her knife, prepared to defend herself against an attack. Elphick observes, "Dystopian authors achieve their goal of reawakening citizens to their own troubled social structure" (172). Here, Elphick discusses the writer/reader relationship in the dystopic text, but the concept applies to Fen's situation. When she regains consciousness, the severity of the situation impacts Fen, and she chastises herself for her human response to exhaustion. Regrettably, her first thoughts are not for her community, which is represented as Baby Girl, but for herself.

While Lydia is alive but Fen is separated from her, Fen is sure of herself and understands what needs to be done in order to protect her leader. Once she renews contact with Lydia, however, Fen appears uncertain and subservient, deferring major decisions to Lydia. Fen behaves in this manner because her identity is in transition, and she continues to need authority figures to help her change into a self-assured adult. When Lydia dies, her education from her tribe has come to an end; this moment also marks Fen's shift in power. Fen is thrust into the caregiver position for the child. She obtains food for the baby and must rely on herself for survival. Even though Fen acknowledges that the tribe no longer exists and she is on her own with the child, she falls back on tribe teachings. These teachings are modified—Fen discards archaic notions about gender and utilizes the knowledge that gives her confidence about her choices.

In her third stage of development, Fen consciously takes action in her society in order to enact change. Both Fen and Daniel have been kidnapped by those wishing to steal their blood; after they meet in captivity, they agree on a trade. Elphick states, "The characters in many critical dystopias painstakingly struggle to *adapt* to and *better* the problems facing them in these texts' microcosmic societies" (173). Whereas Daniel seeks knowledge about the city's layout, Fen wants food, clothing, and an escape from Orleans for Baby Girl. For Fen, taking care of both Baby Girl and Daniel is a required chore. Only once they reach Mr. Go, a family friend, and learn of the liminal state of Orleans does Fen choose to claim the child as her own. Much in the African tradition, Fen waits to name the child until she is in the presence of a community elder, Mr. Go. Her naming the child—Enola after East New Orleans—shows her desire to acknowledge the child as part of her community rather than just as a debt owed to Lydia. When the trio leaves Mr. Go and encounters the O-Negative tribe (the O-Negs), Fen announces to their leader, Davis, that while the child may have been Lydia's, "She mine, now" (Smith ch. 35). In order to show that she refuses to accept her objectified state, Fen chooses to make a public display denouncing it. Similarly, Pulliam documents two of the most renowned open rebellions in *The Hunger Games*, specifically when Katniss grieved for her friend Rue on camera and when she and Peeta attempted suicide (Pulliam 179). In a discussion of race, Leonard refers to this moment in science fiction as "rendering the invisible visible" (257). Fen rebels against her objectification, removing herself from her liminal space once she asserts her power in her meeting with Davis, the head of the O-Negs. Many of Davis's tribe died in the attack on the powwow[2] with the OPs and he wants this debt to be paid with Baby Girl's life. When Fen refuses, she engages in a very public scene, an "open rebellion," and launches herself into the role of tribe leader (Pulliam 179). Davis tries to ensure that Fen remains in her objectified state by referring to her as "Lydia's pet," a slight to which Fen responds with strength. Fen thinks, "I can't help but laugh now. It stupid, me in the middle of this ring, this man calling for blood, when all hell about to break loose. I ain't never been good with fools, and while everything else be changing, that still be the same" (Smith ch. 35). Instead of sacrificing the child, as she tries to do in her second stage of development while they are being chased by dogs, she offers herself (much like Katniss does) as payment for the deaths and fights Davis publicly. She allows him to win for appearance's sake, and, as a result, she saves the trio from death. Fen's ultimate sacrifice, however, comes when she chooses to save her child's life over her own.

Fen comes to the realization that there is no place safe for this child, who is not valued in this space as anything but a commodity, so she has Daniel take Baby Girl over the Wall. In an interview about *Kindred*, the foremost female neo-slave narrative, Octavia E. Butler discussed the enslaved's escape with Nick DiCharrio (206–7). DiCharrio asked Butler about her choice to set *Kindred* in a border state, to which she responded, "Because I wanted my character to have a legitimate hope of escape" (206). Like Butler, Smith places her novel in a border state, making a route to freedom possible for a fortunate few. In reference to the critical dystopia, Elphick states, "There is a sense of hope and unity in these novels that has kept it apart from the despair engulfing the classic dystopias" (173). Both Butler and Smith elect to save the characters that represent the possibility for a favorable future. During the escape, Fen draws attention away from Daniel and Baby Girl: she takes Daniel's coat, which she forms to look like the baby's body, and runs screaming through the moat toward the soldiers. The image of the escaping slave appears repeatedly throughout Smith's text, calling to mind the image of the slave fleeing pursuing slave hunters toward freedom, wading through water in order to flee pursuing masters and/or fugitive slave hunters, but Smith uses Fen to create a new image. Daniel and the child reach freedom while Fen is repeatedly shot; through her ultimate ruse, she enables her child to reach the plague-free Outer States. In a twist to the traditional slave narrative structure, Fen is depicted running in the direction of the soldiers. Fen chooses her own version of freedom—she elects to die by the hand of the soldiers while saving her community rather than succumb to the plague. To the soldiers, Fen is only a body, another sufferer of the plague. In actuality, Fen regains control of her commodified body and chooses to surrender her life in exchange for her child's freedom. In slave narratives, the enslaved's escape is the pivotal moment. Smith uses both the standard escape closing from the slave narrative and the critical dystopian ending to close the novel. She leaves her readers with the image of resistance, of Enola "waving her small fists at the weeping sky," the resilience of the next generation, and the symbol of the fight to escape oppression still to come (Smith ch. 45). As the text closes, the audience comes to the realization that the enslaved's journey to freedom depicted here is not just that of Fen, but also of the next generation, that of Enola.

Just as Smith's *Orleans* tracked Fen's own neo-slave narrative, Sandler's young adult novel *Tankborn* documents a female protagonist's—Kayla's—journey from oppression to freedom, following her escape from socially endorsed enslavement. In a discussion of Butler's *Kindred* and Gayl Jones's *Corregidora*, both novels that emphasize the effects of familial enslavement on their protagonists, Beaulieu observes, "These authors work like archeologists, attempting to uncover the secrets of the past, sometimes to instruct heroines who are confused about their present and unsure of their future" (142). In reference to the most famous neo-slave narratives from female writers, Madhu Dubey states, "What distinguishes [Toni] Morrison's and Butler's uses of this genre is their focus on black women's unique experience of reproductive slavery" (164). Sandler's novel follows Kayla's origin story: during childhood, scientists transform Kayla from a physically challenged child into one who is genetically engineered. In order for Kayla to reach stage three of her development she must, much as former slaves have depicted in narratives, document her knowledge of her origins. By uncovering the truth of her trueborn origins, Kayla determines that Loki is a false utopia and, through this revelation, destabilizes the social constructs that place beings in a discriminatory hierarchal society. In stage one, however, Kayla appears in her socially constructed familial space awaiting her Assignment in the trueborn sector.

Scholars have criticized science fiction literature for its failure to clearly identify the ethnicity of its protagonists even in neo-slave narratives, a shortcoming partially evidenced in Smith's ambiguity about Fen's race. On one hand, Rushdy (*Neo-Slave Narratives*) argues that during the 1960s writers created a new genre, the neo-slave narrative, in order to reclaim the slave narrative from White writers, thereby ensuring that the authentic African American experience may be shown. On the other hand, Mary J. Couzelis notes that in science fiction, race tends to be either ignored, thereby placing preference on whiteness, or depicted as existing singularly. Couzelis writes, "Novels that ignore race or present a monochromatic future imply that other ethnicities do not survive in the future or that their participation in the future is not important" (131). Unlike Smith, who only hints at Fen's ethnicity, Sandler places race in the foreground as she introduces Kayla and Jal. When the text opens, Kayla is objectified by certain members of Lokian society and by the community's precepts. By describing Jal as "her slender, black-skinned nurture brother," the narrator instantly emphasizes race and nonstandard familial relations (Sandler ch. 1). Kayla is Black, female, and GEN. While Kayla's status as a enslaved person is not directly stated upon the text's opening, she is immediately cast as the slave mother character.

In the first stage of her development, Kayla is objectified: she is the commodified body. Historically, enslaved people were seen as having value and were considered property, much like GENs are. Each GEN has a "sket," a skill set incorporated into their genetic makeup while in the tank; Kayla's is her excessive physical strength. In the American slaveholding South, both female and male enslaved people were expected to be physical laborers. By emphasizing Kayla's physical abilities, Sandler draws a parallel between GENs and African American enslaved people. Unlike her best friend, Mishalla, who is described as having the nurturer sket, Kayla has been built for physical labor. On her Thirdday holiday, Tala, Kayla's nurture-mother, directs Kayla to watch Jal. As Kayla describes her duties, her familial structure, and her religious studies, she shows that she is not permitted to have a normal adolescence. She is, instead, thrust into the role of slave mother. While Jal gets to play, Kayla tends to him rather than spending time with her companions. While it may appear like a task required in ordinary adolescence, a female looking after a child, this image of the female pressed into service leans toward the stereotypical behavior of the slave mother. Kayla is placed in this role, defined not by her individual identity but by her race, gender, and class. When the Earth is deemed a wasteland, people moved to Loki in an effort to start again; unfortunately, they brought their caste system with them in an effort to re-create their former society (Elphick 184). Kayla does not get the opportunity to explore who she could become. Instead, societal members with status deem her imperfect, place her in the tank, and alter her body. Those with rank choose her life for her.

It must be noted that critical examination of young adult literature featuring African American characters is lacking. There is, however, one exception. With the rise in popularity of *The Hunger Games*, examinations of both Rue and Katniss have been prevalent. Meghan Gilbert-Hickey examines Rue's district, noting the similarities to the antebellum American South. Rue resides in District Eleven, an area concentrated on agriculture, "where the children miss school during the harvest and workers are publically whipped for eating the crops" (Gilbert-Hickey 12). Subsequently, the district's characters evoke images of field slaves. In *Tankborn*, even though the GENs' Chadi sector does not appear to contain a specific industry, it is reminiscent of the Jim Crow South. Its industry is, in fact, the readying of GENs for Assignment; this preparation includes ensuring that GENs are conditioned to understand their position in Lokian society. Throughout the novel, GENs are often segregated from the rest of the Lokian populace. For example, while Kayla and Jal are by the Chadi River, it becomes clear that the river separates the poverty-stricken Chadi sector from wealthy Foresthill, the trueborn sector. While working for Zul Manel, her trueborn master, Kayla is required to stand in a marked section of a clothing store, away from other castes but always in full view of everyone. She is also required to ride in the back of motor vehicles, just as in the Jim Crow South.

The Chadi sector and the river are the first symbols in the novel of people forcefully separated by space. The GENs live in their own sector but, according to Kayla, it is not safe even though they are permitted to be there. They must constantly live in fear of racial violence from the trueborns. As Kayla grows wary of the trueborns' presence near their sector, she calls for Jal to move away from the river. Unfortunately, he does not comprehend Kayla's warning about impending violence and refuses, thereby placing them both in danger. As in the American antebellum South and Lokian society, it is irrelevant whether or not an enslaved person errs, that person is punished regardless. The GENs are conditioned to adhere to societal guidelines for their caste, and if any are violated, their personalities may be erased. Their bodies may be recycled and used to create other GENs. In other words, a violation of behavioral guidelines or a false accusation of such an act may result in literal, or figurative, death for GENs. In order to transform from object to subject, Kayla must put aside her fear of reprisal and become a leader for her people.

Although Kayla has little power in her society, in her role of slave mother, she proves adaptable and fights to safeguard her people despite her disadvantaged status. While Kayla is objectified in Lokian society—she is considered to be powerless—she also exists as the slave mother, there to protect her community. Even though Kayla believes in ensuring that the statutes regarding GENs are not violated, she sees her nurture brother in danger and acts. In reference to Butler's

Parable, Elphick documents the religion, Earthseed, that Lauren creates and how it "places the individual's ability to adapt to his world as the ultimate power" (188). Once Kayla witnesses the trueborn Livot injure Jal with a rock, she prays to the GEN god, the Infinite, and puts herself in harm's way by running to aid Jal. She also proceeds to verbally insist that Jal flee from incoming danger. As with the slave mother figure, Kayla's first thought is of protection for her community. Unfortunately, Kayla's heroic act is tainted by the narrator's description of the next steps she takes to save Jal. Instead of focusing on Kayla's selfless act, the reader's attention is placed on Kayla's nonhuman qualities—the animal DNA, which makes her extremely strong and links her to the stereotype of the enslaved person as being animalistic.

Throughout slave narratives, enslaved people are repeatedly documented as being treated as chattel. In *Narrative of the Life of Frederick Douglass, an American Slave,* Douglass writes about his return to the plantation in Talbot County, Maryland, in order to be valued after the death of his "master." Here, Douglass delineates how the enslaved people are placed alongside the farm's livestock as both are categorized as property. Throughout this quintessential slave narrative, Douglass repeatedly compared the enslaved person's existence to that of an animal's in order to reinforce the notion that the enslaved were looked upon as animalistic and also to promote the need for a reclassification of enslaved persons as human beings rather than property. Although Kayla steps in, physically takes hold of Jal, and proceeds to carry him ashore when trueborn Devak Manel prevents his friend, Livot, from tossing another projectile at Jal, Sandler's description of Kayla's animalistic state undermines her heroism and agency. While Kayla's behavior may look heroic—she is protecting Jal from physical injury and/or death—this impression is short-lived. The narrator notes, "The bank was steep enough she had to pull herself up on all fours, but as usual the hyper-genned strength of her upper body got the better of her lower. She fumbled more than once, muddying her knees, adding to the ugly ankle-high sludge staining her best leggings" (Sandler ch. 1). Kayla is portrayed as animalistic and uncoordinated. Before she maneuvers Jal out of the river, the two trueborns converse about Kayla's animal DNA, indicating their belief that she is partially porcine. As Kayla is in stage one of her development, she is objectified by both the trueborns and the narrator. The description of Kayla's heroic act is disparaging, her act of rebellion repressed and overshadowed by her analogy to a brute, another stock trait of the slave stereotype. Before Devak gets too close, Kayla informs Jal that he must go to their residence and, if she does not arrive later, tell their nurture-mother, Tala, where she has been. Kayla acts as a leader once more, protecting her community, before she reverts to her former objectified self and loses her power. Once Devak arrives in front of her, the comparisons regarding her appearance begin and her oppression continues.

A certain appearance is shown to be preferred among the characters in Sandler's novel. While physical whiteness does not appear to be predominant, it continues to permeate Kayla's society. Upon meeting Devak, Kayla looks him over appraisingly and then herself disparagingly. First, she admires Devak's "straight and glossy" hair while criticizing hers for being "wild and kinked"; she also includes Jal's "tight curls" in her description of appearance, a trait unsuitable in Loki, as it indicates GEN association (Sandler ch. 1). She splits traits into two groups: those that belong to trueborns and those that identify GENs (which, therefore, the majority considers undesirable). Devak's skin is described as "the perfect color, a rich medium brown. Not near black like Jal's, nor the pale mud color of her own skin, but a warm shade in between. The color of status" (Sandler ch. 1). Devak is neither White nor Black, thereby symbolically shown as inhabiting an in-between space. Devak and other trueborns are able to travel to any sector, their travel permits existing in the form of the body. Trueborns' complexions and ornate ear balis reveal their status to others, ensuring freedom of movement even as appearance hinders movement for other castes.

In the "Author's Note" that follows *Tankborn*, Sandler imparts the origins of the novel, stating that first it was a screenplay; however, when it was not produced, she revised the text, turning it into a novel (Sandler). Specifically, Sandler retained Kayla and the GENs' characters, but the "caste system crept in, inspired by my long-ago conversations with an Indian-born co-worker" ("Author's Note"). Sandler attempts to call attention to the plight of many oppressed peoples, but the inclusion of too many obscures her point by making it appear that all oppressed people have the same experiences, which is untrue. Devak, who may represent a person of Indian descent, has his appearance designated as ideal by Kayla. Kayla disparages her own appearance, which resembles that of a person of African descent, and focuses her comments mainly on hair and complexion. The remarks that Kayla makes about her appearance are primarily within her mind, showing how her oppressed state leads to self-hatred and loss of voice. Kayla fleetingly wonders about the differing appearances of humans on Loki, noting her GEN friend Beela's physical traits and their similarities to those of the trueborns.

Though Fen and Kayla both free themselves from their objectified states in the end, the process of doing so for Kayla requires more developmental stages than it did for Fen. Fen's first stage of development includes the identification of the objectified state; subsequently, in stage two, she unconsciously takes action to remove herself from her oppressed state. Unlike Fen, Kayla does not take action to free herself from oppression until her third stage. During Kayla's first stage of development, she acts to protect Jal, but not to remove him or herself from the objectified state. Even though Kayla violates social codes by defending Jal, speaking with Devak, and questioning her origins, she is still immersed in an oppressed community. When offered her first Assignment, Kayla begrudgingly accepts it, thereby continuing the practice of the GEN as enslaved. Notably, if Kayla had refused her Assignment, she could have been reset or murdered. When she accepts, doubt creeps into her mind before being forcefully separated from her nurture-family. It is pushed aside by her devotion to the GEN god: "She knew it was the Infinite's will, that a GEN's trial of servitude was the only way back to His hands" (Sandler ch. 2). This god, unbeknown to Kayla until her third stage, has been created in order to ensure obedience from the GENs to the trueborns and their societal hierarchy. For Kayla, as with many enslaved people, religion offers strength. Even when it is revealed that her god is created as a method of control, Kayla continues to worship, thereby revealing that she refuses to be dominated. Trites, in reference to power, states that there is a "relationship between discourse and action" (*Disturbing* 48). In her mind, Kayla protests by expressing distaste for her societal guidelines, creating a solitary discourse; by doing so, she acknowledges that the hierarchy is flawed. Despite its flaws, however, she retreats into prayer, refusing to take action and repressing her rebellious spirit due to her fear of reprisal. In front of Tala and Jal, Kayla verbally asserts her loathing for the trueborns, but only when she is safely within the domestic space; once she is removed, she is alone among those that see her as inferior.

    In the second stage of her transition, Kayla is offered illegal information from the rebels while she is in her domestic space, but it is in front of a GEN enforcer. At this point, Kayla does not know that Skal is a member of the resistance. In order for information to be transferred to the GENs, a datapod is placed against the GEN's tattoo. The transfer is a symbolic rape. During this transfer, the GEN may lose consciousness, does feel pain, and bleeds from the point of insertion. Even though Kayla knows Skal, he is a GEN enforcer and cannot be trusted. When uploaded, the information from the Kinship—the rebels who desire equality in Loki—informs her that there is a mysterious packet that she must hide. Debra Walker King, in *African Americans and the Culture of Pain*, documented multiple moments during lynchings of African Americans when the men elected to remain silent. King conveys, "Silence emerges as a defensive strategy, a mobility that allows torture victims some control over the way they experience and navigate pain and racial hurt. It is a way of rising above victimization, if only symbolically" (93). Once Kayla receives the message, she debates within herself its authenticity. She does not verbalize that she has received a message from the rebellion, nor does she tell anyone about the packet of information she is to protect. When she cannot find the packet in her bag, she dismisses the message until after Tanti is reset. Once Jal's friend, Tanti, is realigned by enforcer Ansgar for doing something as harmless as touching his datapod, Kayla begins to take more chances with her life and for her freedom. When Kayla locates the packet of information, she unconsciously takes action toward her freedom. At this time Kayla is unaware that the packet is from the Kinship, but she is still willing to conceal it stitched into a pair of her leggings. When she goes on Assignment, Kayla brings this packet to the trueborn sector. Importantly, Kayla becomes the caregiver for Zul, Devak's grandfather. It is Zul that is the leader of the rebellion and who also assisted in creating the GENs. He is able to offer Kayla information about her origins that she lacks.

At the Manel house, Kayla continues on her journey to the subjective position; in order to enact change in her society, Kayla must first obtain information that she will use to alter her own perspective regarding her place in Lokian society. Kayla cares for the elderly Zul, who, unbeknown to her, unwillingly aided in the creation of the GENs and is a founder of the Kinship. Here, Sandler alludes to the enslaver/enslaved's relationship prevalent in slave narratives. In the traditional slave narrative, the narrator recounts many instances in which false information has been transmitted to enslaved people; this information is not discounted because the enslaved, due to illiteracy, are unable to do so. Repeatedly in the novel, GENs assert the rumor that if a GEN touches a trueborn, then the GEN will be injured. In her neo-slave narrative, Sandler addresses the master/slave relationship from a new standpoint: Zul is the contrite, heroic figure for whom Kayla has sympathy. Because of this relationship, many myths are debunked—the GEN creation story and the establishment of the caste system—which results in Kayla defying the ruling authority's guidelines. The body becomes a site of resistance that enables Kayla's rebellious acts. According to King, in order to secure survival for their children, African American mothers in literature often relinquish a part of their bodies. In particular, King referred to Toni Morrison's Sethe's loss of mother's milk and Eva Peace's leg ("Writing" 61). In *Tankborn*, Kayla touches Zul without gloves and finds that there are no ill effects; later, Kayla verbally asserts to Devak that she is a human as he is. Kayla gives up the false beliefs regarding GENs instilled in her. Both aforementioned acts show that unconsciously her behavior regarding her enslavement is changing and she is headed toward freedom for herself.

In the third stage of her development, Kayla consciously acts to free herself from her forced confinement. As subject, Kayla chooses to take action that will, inevitably, change her society's caste system. Kayla's friend, Mishalla, is kidnapped by those, including Director Manel, who steal children in order to change them into GENs. Zul requests that Devak illegally enter the GEN monitoring grid and that Kayla assist him. At this point, Kayla has been used to store data regarding the Kinship's uprising; she rightfully questions Zul's placing the information within her without her permission. She also accepts the task of illegally entering Director Manel's office and aids Devak in doing so in order to obtain the information needed to find Mishalla and the missing children. Once Kayla understands that she and other trueborn children who have been born with physical challenges are being transformed into GENs, she consciously chooses to assist the resistance. Kayla both voices her idea for breaking down the door to Mishalla's prison and completes the physical act. After Director Manel and his associates have been arrested and the stolen children returned to their families, Kayla officially joins the resistance in order to locate any other missing children. As in the slave narrative, Kayla is last witnessed freed from enslavement and on her way to assisting others to break free as well.

Through their activism, both Fen and Kayla assist in securing freedom for future generations. When Fen is shown in her objectified state, she seems strong-willed and independent but not community-minded. Stereotypically, the slave mother thinks more about the community, sacrificing herself in the process in the same way Lydia risks her health to care for the dying. Fen does not verbally reprimand Lydia about her actions, thinking, "No use telling her she a fool for being here when she carrying a new life and her time being so close" (Smith ch. 1). Fen's parents show her how to protect herself, but only herself. Lydia teaches Fen not only to care for others through her ministering to the dying but also to make choices that serve her community well. Through her parents and Lydia's teachings, which she applies while caring for Baby Girl, Fen transitions from adolescent to community leader. Her consciously chosen act of self-sacrifice, her life for Baby Girl's, reveals her desire to protect the Orleans society and to ensure its survival. When the novel concludes, both Fen and Baby Girl are depicted as enslaved people freed from societal objectification. In her own way, by embracing her ability to choose, even Fen escapes her state of bondage.

In *Tankborn*, Kayla is born into enslavement, her societal ideology engrained into her identity. Kayla is discontent in her objectified state but is powerless to alter it until she obtains knowledge from the rebellion. Once she enters her second stage of development, Kayla fluctuates between rebelliousness and compliance. During the third stage of her development, Kayla discovers that there is a cure for being a GEN; if taken, the GEN will transform into a human. In a discussion of what she termed "identity politics," Trites states, "Those who rebel against the mores of their social class are still identified in terms of the institution they are rejecting: their behavior as rebels is defined in terms of what they reject about social class as an institution" (*Disturbing* 46). Kayla, rather than take it herself, elects to give the antidote to Mishalla, thereby remaining a GEN. Even though not taking the cure means that she cannot move from her state of bondage, she chooses the freedom of another over her own. Through her act of electing to remain a GEN, Kayla shows that she not only embraces her identity but also that she is willing to work as an activist, helping to transform her society into one that values equality instead of intolerance and the community over the individual. By emphasizing both the community and the individual, Fen and Kayla reveal themselves to be true leaders. In authentic critical dystopian style, Smith and Sandler conclude their respective novels by hinting to their readers the possibility for future societal change in Fen's and Kayla's communities (Elphick 173). It is the science fictional critical dystopia that allows readers to see adolescents as powerful, as enacting change in their respective communities. Unfortunately, science fiction texts featuring African American female characters still appear infrequently. When they do, the characters tend to have minor roles, their plotlines buried behind that of the White characters. While both Smith's and Sandler's character portrayals could have been improved by placing more emphasis on ethnicity, they have brought attention to the field of twenty-first-century young adult science fiction.

Chapter 2

THE SAFETY OF SPACE IN NNEDI OKORAFOR'S *THE BOOK OF PHOENIX* AND *BINTI*

Young adult science fiction featuring female protagonists of color is still relatively uncommon as is scholarship about this area. With the advent of the twenty-first century, however, fiction featuring not only protagonists of color but also female leads appear to be increasing (slowly). Writer Nnedi Okorafor has significantly contributed to the areas of both Afrofuturism and YA literature with her body of work. Her novels and her Binti series novellas revolve around an exceptional adolescent female of African descent. The novelist's Nigerian background is reflected in her characters' composition. Okorafor has her female protagonist venture on the traditional quest of exploration, so that she may establish her identity. Throughout her journey, the female protagonist places great emphasis on her attachment to space and community. In an homage to J. G. Ballard's novel *High Rise*, Okorafor creates *The Book of Phoenix* (*BP*; 2016). This novel was written as a prequel to her award-winning novel *Who Fears Death* (2015), which occurs in Nigeria after the fall of Phoenix's society. Phoenix, the two-year-old narrator, resides in Tower 7, a self-sustained environment. Phoenix is categorized as a speciMEN, "'an accelerated organism,' born two years ago" (Okorafor, *BP* ch. 1). In keeping with the neo-slave narrative structure, emphasis is placed upon the Black female body, especially the objectification of Phoenix by the corporation, what she and other speciMEN term the "Big Eye." As Phoenix offers a definition of a speciMEN, she also calls attention to the stages of both her physical and her mental maturation: "Yet I looked and physically felt like a forty-year-old woman" (*BP* ch. 1). Okorafor continues her tradition of utilizing a first-person narrator in *Phoenix*;

here, Phoenix intimates that her mental and physical maturity are out of sync. The artificial maturation that her body has experienced does not match her actual mental and emotional development. In order to discover the secret of her origins and the reason for the suicide of her friend Saaed, Phoenix must explore the tower, a place she considers to be her home but also her space of forced confinement.

In *Binti* (2015), the protagonist of the same name ventures away from her home in order to attend Oomza University, a prestigious learning institution located on another planet. The issue is that Binti leaves without the support of her community. Her people, the Himba (Earth), do not leave their space in the desert. The Himba are not stagnant in their development; rather their sense of self is heavily influenced by their space. In fact, Binti is the first of her species to be accepted to and attend the university (she goes on a spaceship); she is also the first to leave her people. Throughout the novella, Okorafor stresses the importance of space and how, alluding to the African tradition of doing so, Binti draws courage from her people, her culture, and her homeland. Many of Okorafor's texts, including the ones chosen for this study, may be considered neo-slave narratives. While a specific place offers safety for many, for others there is a dire need to escape. Whether an area may be considered a space (no emotional attachment to it), or a place (emotional attachment to it), the culture linked to it influences both Phoenix and Binti, thereby aiding in their emotional development.

As Smith does with *Orleans*, Okorafor begins *The Book of Phoenix* with the authenticating voice. In Stepto's delineation of the slave narrative structure, he discusses the reason this voice appears in the text. Stepto reports that "their primary function is, of course, to authenticate the former slave's account; in doing so, they are at least partially responsible for the narrative's acceptance as historical evidence" (3). For Smith, the narrator of the "Before" section is a third-person unknown narrator. This character is intimately familiar with the state of predystopian New Orleans but does not appear as part of the plot involving Fen, thereby affecting the text's outcome. The voice is there ultimately for the reader's benefit, thereby offering an insider's glimpse into the city's prehurricane conditions. Here, the narrator follows trumpet player Edmund Brossard's purposeful walk through the French Market, a journey taken even though the hurricane warning has been given signaling imminent disaster. The "Before" narrator's task is to capture what appears to be a fleeting moment in time but, in actuality, documents the resilience of the people of New Orleans. This section has been included not to verify the validity of Fen's account but rather the spirit of the residents of New Orleans. In other words, while the circumstances may change as do the parties involved, their desire to persevere does not. The "Before" section exists, as Stepto has written, "as historical evidence" regarding the legitimacy of the narrative as a whole and conforms to the authenticating narrative structure (Stepto 5). Stepto observes, "The tale is *subsumed by the authenticating strategy*; the slave narrative becomes an authenticating document for other, usually generic, texts, e.g., novels, histories" (5). In keeping with Stepto's construction of the slave narrative, Okorafor's *The Book of Phoenix* is framed within the authenticating Prologue and Epilogue. For Smith's narrative, the "Before" section never overpowers Fen's story, instead it contributes to the reader's understanding of Fen's persistence. In reference to Brossard, Smith's narrator states, "He was not leaving his home. New Orleans would stand against any storm that came her way" ("Before"). The "Before" section, specifically that which concentrates on Brossard, allows for a transmission of information about a populace joined together by local pride of place. It is not until the government documents are inserted between the Brossard account in "Before" and Fen's in "After" that the outsider's voice interferes with the harmony offered by the community of New Orleans. To Broussard and those that remained under threat of imminent disaster, New Orleans is "home," a concept that Phoenix is rarely offered, even though she asserts in the opening of the narrative that Tower 7 is, in fact, that very same thing to her.

In Phoenix's society, which is reminiscent of that from the cyberpunk genre, the private corporation dominates the landscape and controls the lives of its citizens. Before Phoenix's narrative begins, an unnamed narrator tells the story of how Sunuteel, an Okeke man, discovers a cache of technology in a cave; Okorafor labels this section "Prologue: Found." In reference to neo-slave narratives, Paula T. Connolly writes that they "recover otherwise lost voices, but as they do so, they reframe conventions of the antebellum slave narrative" (199–200). For Fen, the "Before" section contributes to the reader's overall understanding of the community in Orleans, that which is made up of both people that remember New Orleans as it was previous to the erection of the wall and those who have lived their lives segregated from what remains of America. The protagonist has no control over her creation by the scientists at the Big Eye corporation, but by recording her story, Phoenix gives herself the opportunity to take control of her life. The narrative is a safe space, one in which Phoenix may divulge her secrets. Her first-person narration permits a candid self-reflection that prevails over others seeking her silence, her conformity to a system that enslaved her. For Phoenix, whose life has been meticulously planned since before conception, the narrative itself presents the protagonist and the audience with insights regarding her mysterious origins. The calculating narrator of the Prologue, however, offers clarity about the desert people's background, one that no longer villainizes the Okeke for altering the landscape. Connolly continues, "Authenticating letters that prefaced and appended antebellum slave narratives and were typically authored by white abolitionists to assure readers of the text's veracity are exchanged in neo-slave narratives" (200). In Okorafor's novel, the Prologue is updated to reflect its futuristic setting. The letter is not a representation of a written work but, instead, appears to be a recording, something that may be played on a "portable." In Sunuteel's space, the portable is utilized as a way to access information and as a means of communication. This is not to say that it is the preferred method of transmitting information, as that remains the verbal communiqué of the story.

In the West African tradition, the griot remains a significant member of the community, as this person retains historical information, later transmitting it to the community in an act of communal bonding. Traditionally, as in West African works such as *Sunjata*, the griot utilizes the call-and-response model, thereby involving the audience in the story being told. In *The Book of Phoenix*, Sunuteel acts as the griot as he has located Phoenix's prerecorded story and passed it on to future generations. As with many origin stories, the narrator implies that many believe that the story has been sent by a god, specifically Ani, the Igbo mother goddess. The Prologue is not being told by

Sunuteel, however, but by the unnamed non-African narrator. In reference to the authentication process contained within the neo-slave narrative, Connolly writes that "framing documents—often an author's note or bibliography—cite slave narratives or slave studies as sources, thus reclaiming the slave's voice as the only necessary authentication for accounts about slavery" (200). Opening the text, Okorafor's acknowledgments are the traditional writer's thanks to others for their help. The quotation that Okorafor has included from poet Robert Hayden's "Middle Passage" is another story. Hayden documents the harrowing journey of enslaved people from Africa to America, observing that their mortality is tested on board and continues to be once they reach land. By prefacing her novel with the poetic lines and dedicating it "To the stolen girls of Chibock, Nigeria," Okorafor places emphasis on enslavement, thereby making the connection to Phoenix's story clear. Summarizing Stepto's authenticating structure, Jermaine O. Archer writes that it "occurs when an author, like William Wells Brown, is able to make the text an authenticating document for other generic narratives" (78). In other words, while the Prologue and Epilogue appear to belong to the eclectic narrative—White voices designed to control the Black voice within—in actuality, Phoenix's voice dominates the story and ensures that the narrator's doubts are discounted.

Upon the Prologue's opening, the narrator is unnamed, but it may be determined that the voice is not the same as that which closes the text, that of Sola. While this voice offers its views on the origins of the Great Book, it is skeptical that the writer of the book is a mortal, the voice preferring instead to give its origins as divine. The Prologue's narrator offers the Great Book's provenance as one similar to that of the Koran. According to the narrator, "Most believe that the Great Book's author was a mad yet holy, always always holy, prophet who'd taken refuge in a cave" (Okorafor, *BP* Prologue). The narrator qualifies origin statements made about the Great Book by telling the story of Sunteel and his wife, Hussaina. This couple is elderly and nomadic, preferring to make the desert their home. Hussaina's people have an Islamic background, but Hussaina's religious preference is unclear. The narrator implies that lightening sets a tree on fire (the proverbial burning bush, which happens to appear like a woman on fire) so that Sunuteel may wander and Hussaina has a moment of contemplation. Whereas authenticating narratives tend to be written by, or include the voice of, the formerly enslaved person, what Stepto calls the "eclectic narrative" has Caucasian voices attached to the narrative itself. In the eclectic narrative, the formerly enslaved person's story tends to be buried beneath that of the authenticating documents and their story undercut by those who have been included to verify the narrative's accuracy. In reference to Booker T. Washington's *Up from Slavery*, Stepto examines the inclusion of the authenticating texts, observing that "Once assembled, these documents not only authenticate Washington's tale, but also, because they have been edited and contextualized within the tale, enhance Washington's authorial control" (Stepto 41). The narrators of the Prologue and Epilogue do not undermine Phoenix's story, even though Sola attempts to do so. Rather, the Prologue's speaker offers the various versions of the Great Book's origin and then allows the duo's story to unfold. The purpose is not to place emphasis on the abolitionist's story over that of the enslaved person but, instead, to document Sunuteel's position and expertise as a griot before proceeding with Phoenix's narrative, one of which it has been noted is part of the Great Book. In keeping with the authenticating narrative construction, the Prologue contains Phoenix's voice introducing both her mode of storytelling—"To tell my tale, I will use the old African tools of story: Spoken words"—and the objectification of the speciMEN and the scientists (Okorafor, *BP* Prologue). By including Phoenix's own statements, which lead into the narrative itself, the focus is not on the unnamed narrator or Sunuteel but on Phoenix's journey to freedom from enslavement. It is Phoenix that is in control of this text and of the primary mode of information transmission.

In fact, first-person narration appears to be Okorafor's preferred method as she utilizes it in her earlier works "Hello, Moto" (2011) and the Akata series (2011 and 2017) and the later Binti series. In her Tor.com short story "Hello, Moto," Rain accepts the role of storyteller as she must relate what has happened to her friends, Philo and Coco, and herself. In the story's Preface (the section given in italics before she reflects on previous events), Rain speaks in definitives only when she refers to events that occurred between her friends and herself.

When discussing the conclusion of those catastrophic actions, Rain is ambiguous, appearing to instead prefer possibilities—in other words, she leaves the ending up to the reader's imagination. After introducing her story, Rain directs the listener to *"Walk with me. This is the story of How the Smart Woman Tried to Right Her Great Wrong"* (Okorafor, "Hello, Moto"). Her Preface, like that from *Phoenix*, begins with a quotation significant to her protagonist's plight. The statement from Nobel Laureate Wangari Maathai stresses acceptance for African females and freedom from seeing themselves as Other, notably "liberat[ion] from fear and from silence" ("Hello, Moto"). Rain, who uses her technological expertise combined with juju, asserts that she creates three wigs in the desire for the female community to assist others. Her misguided effort to conform to what she believes is the societal norm—the covering of natural hair with wigs designed to represent Caucasian hair—causes her to create the wigs, which bring out negative qualities in the women. Rain uses her Prologue as a space in which to comment on the state of her unnamed African society and the behavior of its female inhabitants. To her audience Rain says, *"The wigs were supposed to make things better. But something went wrong. Like the nation we were trying to improve, we became backward. Instead of giving, we took"* ("Hello, Moto"). Here, Rain shows that she attempted to bypass her own culture, thereby emulating that of the Western colonizer, which is physically represented as the wig. As with *The Book of Phoenix*, "Hello, Moto" contains a society where Africa and its people are used as resources and a protagonist who must attempt to accept her own culture rather than another's. In the conclusion of the story, as the characters are transformed into vampires, Rain reveals that the women have already been affected but leaves the ending somewhat open-ended. Okorafor makes it clear that contact with Western concepts forever changed her trio, but as Rain is aware of the mistake she has made, preferring another culture over her own, she is able to remedy this issue. She closes the story trying to stop her friends from further harming her society; Phoenix's story will also end in violence for her story and a symbolic cleansing.

In the Epilogue, a Caucasian man named Sola closes the text, seemingly not debasing Phoenix's story but rather that of Sunuteel. Sola does attempt to recast events as he sees fit, trying to dominate the text with his voice. Connolly states that "Neo-slave narratives focus on the subjectivity of slaves in their recovery or fictive re-creation of the slave's perspective" (400). Sola criticizes Sunuteel's ability and position as a griot, his wife's as a seer, subsequently denouncing the Great Book as a version of real events containing an interpretation of Phoenix's story. According to Sola, "The old African man took the bones, blood, and quivering flesh of Phoenix's book, digested its marrow and defecated a tale of his own" (Okorafor, *BP* Epilogue). Recasting Phoenix's story in this fashion, as only containing elements of the truth, Sola attempts to undermine her journey from object to subject. In reference to the "prefatory and appended letters" as well as the standard structure for the slave narrative, James Olney writes that one reason for their attachment was the verification of the actual existence of the former slave (155). By accusing Sunuteel of altering the story, Sola tries to discount Phoenix's identity, thereby attempting to disprove the existence of Phoenix herself. The slave narrative structure also consists of, according to Olney, the attached documents so that the authenticity of the autobiography may be established, but that existence must be proven before truthfulness (155). While Sola attempts to destabilize the Great Book by placing doubt within the mind of the reader, the evidence to the contrary undermines his attempt. Before he denounces Sunuteel and Phoenix's stories, Sola states, "I am a white man; I have and I use the privilege of unhindered mobility. I laugh because most of my words are lies" (Okorafor, *BP* Epilogue). While Olney asserts that the appendix tends to comprise texts that the abolitionists would have seen as giving weight to the legitimacy of the narrative, he also determines that both the close of the narrative and the appendix include "reflections on slavery" (53). Sola's Epilogue is just that, but not from an antienslavement standpoint. By disparaging Sunuteel and Phoenix, Sola as the figurative slaveholder endeavors to retake control of the body—the narrative being the metaphorical body of the enslaved person. As Phoenix's narrative contains anecdotal information about the Big Eye, the White-controlled corporation, Sola is unable to reclaim Phoenix's already freed body.

As Okorafor has followed the structure of the slave narrative but adjusted it to fit neo-slave narrative conventions, Phoenix's story does not include "a first sentence beginning, 'I was born . . . ,' then specifying a place but not a date of birth" (Olney 153). Instead, Phoenix begins by focusing her narrative on space, in particular Tower 7. Before she asserts her space and the fact that she considered the tower both a "prison" and a "home," she gives her story a title and documents her growth. Phoenix says, "I call my story The Book of Phoenix. It is reliable and short, because it was accelerated. . . ." (Okorafor, *BP* Prologue). Stepto observes that by inserting the voice of the former enslaved person in the authenticating documents, the control of the overall text shifts from the White abolitionists in the eclectic narrative to that of the former enslaved person in the authenticating structure. In reference to the title of Frederick Douglass's iconic narrative, Olney writes, "There is much more to the phrase 'written by himself,' of course, than the mere laconic statement of a fact: it is literally a part of the narrative, becoming an important thematic element in the retelling of the life wherein literary, identity, and a sense of freedom are all acquired simultaneously and without the first, according to Douglass, the latter two would never have been" (156). Like Douglass's, Phoenix's narrative is her own; however, it has been updated to reflect the technological advances. In a manner similar to that of Douglass's famed narrative, Phoenix names hers after herself, paralleling the slave narrative's designation "written by himself." At the close of the Prologue, Phoenix relates a small selection about her birth and her life, preferring instead to wait until after she establishes her residency and her literacy to tell the reader more about herself.

Olney writes that the title of a slave narrative is contradictory because it denotes freedom and captivity simultaneously (156). Phoenix's story differs from others because she is literate from the start and this literacy adds to her confinement rather than working with her to remove her from her objectified state. She tells her audience that she has been given a tablet preloaded with thousands of books, most of which she has already digested by the age of two. Unlike the traditional slave narrative structure in which the slave finds literary awareness freeing, while she resides in the tower, knowledge through books makes Phoenix's world smaller. For example, a famed literary parallel to Phoenix's experience would be that from Mary Shelley's *Frankenstein*, specifically when the son of Victor Frankenstein reads Frankenstein's journals about his creation. The son comes to the realization that he has been created and subsequently abandoned because he is considered by his creator and society to be an "abomination" (Okorafor, *BP* ch. 1). Phoenix is aware she is considered to be as she categorizes, a being who differs from society's definition of normal, and her delving into her reading materials enhances her knowledge that she differs from others. For Phoenix, knowledge is, indeed, her gateway for escape, for subjectivity, but it is the perceived death of her community—her friend, Saaed—that begins the onset of self-awareness. Until his suicide, which later Phoenix reveals has been falsified so that Saaed may escape the Big Eye, the protagonist willingly submits to the Big Eye. In her childlike state, Phoenix is sheltered and lives in ignorance; she understands that she and the others differ in construction from mild speciMEN and nonmodified humans, but there is no desire to remove herself from the tower and her objectification by the Big Eye. As a child, Phoenix is trusting and unaware of the immorality regarding her treatment, so for a time her only rebellion regarding the Big Eye system is one that is expected under conventional circumstances: Saaed kisses Phoenix in the lunchroom. Once this moment of self-exploration occurs, even though they have been told by one of the guards to stop—"No affected behavior"—Phoenix relates to the listener that they later kiss again (Okorafor, *BP* ch. 1). Once Saaed dies and Phoenix's trust in the Big Eye has been compromised, Phoenix escapes from the tower and subsequently investigates her origins. Before the information about Saaed's suicide comes to light, however, Phoenix must reveal her parentage to the reader. In a slave narrative, after birth and location are asserted, parentage is discussed.

Whereas Okorafor's setting evokes parallels to Ballard's novel, similarities connected to the folk and fairy tale may also be made. The image of the princess in the tower, or as it is more commonly known, the damsel in distress stock character construct, is also summoned. While Phoenix may physically appear to be an adult, her mental age does not match that of her body. Confirming to the slave narrative structure, Phoenix's story begins with an adult version of herself looking back upon her childhood. She does not begin with her birth per standard format but with a description of the tower and its reason for being. Tower 7 is one of the many spaces dedicated to what Phoenix terms research by the Big Eye corporation. Phoenix asserts that until the death of Saaed, "I understood the purpose of Tower 7," but after his death the meaning of the tower forever changed (Okorafor, *BP* ch. 1). According to Karen E. Rowe, in reference to the adolescent female fairy tale protagonist, "She often achieves comforting release from anxieties by subconsciously perceiving in symbolic tales the commonness of her existential dilemma" (328). Before Phoenix states that she has altered her perception of the tower, she observes that she has read extensively about the others in the tower, about various religions, and about different branches of science. She then goes on to tell the listener, "Carrying all this in my head, I understood abomination" (Okorafor, *BP* ch. 1). Because Okorafor's novel is a neo-slave narrative, the princess in the tower trope has more of a sordid background than it previously had. For the fairy tale Rapunzel or the contemporary Princess Peach or Zelda, the female figures wait in their respective towers until the male hero recues them. While Phoenix does as Rowe has stated, metaphorically burying herself in knowledge, she does so only until the perceived demise of Saaed acts as a catalyst urging her to escape her confinement. Before this removal may occur, however, Phoenix must disclose her conception to the listener.

First, Phoenix reveals that she has spent her entire life—she is two years old in the opening—on the twenty-eighth floor of the tower and intimates that she has been enslaved by the Big Eye corporation. She is, in fact, the product of an egg donor from Phoenix, Arizona, and an unknown father; therefore, Phoenix is a futuristic test-tube baby. With regards to her birth, Okorafor is intimating that Phoenix has been born a slave. She has been created to serve the Big Eye corporation, and the means of her conception has been purchased by the corporation; this conception includes the participation of a surrogate to carry Phoenix to term. Connolly elaborates on the neo-slave construction, noting that its form is based on its audience's age (200). In effect, the younger the audience the more the writer alludes to the harsh realities of slavery, especially that which involves violence (Connolly 200–201). In reference to slave and neo-slave narrative picture books, those that are intended for an audience of children, Connolly notes that while the harsh realities of enslavement are implied, the resilience of the community is emphasized (202–3). There is a certain hopefulness asserted in the books for children (203). For the YA audience, however, there is a realism associated with the depictions of enslavement; they tend to contain more explicit imagery rather than glossed over representations (203–5). Connolly also asserts that contained within is "the impossibility of its easy reparation" (203). As a result of Phoenix's method of conception, the scientists believe that they may abuse Phoenix's body through their experimentation as they see fit. For example, after Phoenix accidentally set fire to her room, the Nigerian scientist Bumi places her in what Phoenix refers to as a "furnace" and burns her, noting that her distress will enable them to assist her (Okorafor, *BP* ch. 1). A more experienced Phoenix, looking back on previous events, informs the listener that due to her blind faith in the Big Eye, "I believed her" (Okorafor, *BP* ch. 1). Phoenix's faith in the Big Eye, her illusions about them caring for and about the speciMEN are gone forever once Saaed dies. The community exists intermittently for Phoenix throughout her narrative. As Phoenix embarks on her mission to destroy the Big Eye, she continues her journey of self-exploration, one that leads her to her two mothers.

Traditionally, in a slave narrative the mother, an enslaved woman, may be mentioned but not known well, or at all, by the child, and the father tends to be the child's White enslaver. In her book *Saints, Sinners, and Saviors*, Trudier Harris documents the stereotypes about Black woman stressing those associated with physical appearance and personality. Among others, Harris highlights various incarnations of the mother figure and, critically, "the black female character who was more suprahuman than human, more introspective—indeed, at times, isolated—than involved, more silently working out what she perceived to be the best for her children than actively and warmly communicating those desires to them" (11). As Phoenix delineates her birth and parentage, she informs her listener that she spends her time alone unless the scientists are there studying her. Historically, enslaved African American children were separated from their parents and raised by a surrogate, usually an older enslaved woman. Unlike the other residents of the tower, Phoenix keeps to herself, her only friendship being that with Saaed. For instance, during her visits to the cafeteria, Phoenix acts as an observer because almost all of the other speciMEN regard her as an oddity. Here, Okorafor offers her reader a character that behaves much like a regular adolescent. She is unsure of herself, thereby refraining to associate with the others, and she automatically accepts the scientists' assertions as truth, even after she is shot by one. While in the tower, Phoenix takes on traits similar to those of the super mother figure noted by Harris. To the listener, Phoenix observes that she has above average intelligence and the ability to heat an area to a degree where objects and people in her radius are set on fire; she also sprouts wings. Eventually, Phoenix has the ability to fly across the ocean, thereby reaching other towers in her quest to destroy them and free the speciMEN within. She has been created, as Phoenix believes, not to aid humanity but to destroy those around her.

While Harris's adult mother figure stereotype resembles Phoenix—her physical capabilities and her often lone state—Okorafor refuses to continue to perpetuate the stereotype. While Phoenix may appear physically as an adult female, she is constantly in a state of flux. Unlike the slave narrative that begins with childhood, Phoenix introduces herself as an adolescent in transition. For example, when she accidentally loses control of her ability for the first time, Phoenix does not think about leaving. She is hesitant to rebel against authority until Saaed's death, and then it is her thoughts that show she refuses to conform; while she has studied about the outside world and the mysterious tree in the tower lobby, she does not question remaining until she learns that Saaed has died from eating her apple. Before her maturation begins, she cannot recognize her capabilities; Phoenix internalizes her lack of confidence in herself and her fear of the unknown. It is not until Saaed dies that Phoenix observes her ill treatment, the physical abuses supposedly committed in the name of science that she chooses to investigate the circumstances of Saaed's death, subsequently escaping the tower. While Phoenix may have been created in a laboratory, she metaphorically gives birth to herself when she flees with her friend Mmuo and destroys the tower. She is not ready, however, to meet her female family members until after she reengages with her father figure, and he teaches her about her abilities. It is only once she becomes accustomed to utilizing her gifts that Phoenix meets her two mothers.

With the introduction to the Library of Congress, the receptacle for the Big Eye's confidential records regarding their experiments,

Phoenix obtains clues to her parentage. As she scours the Tower Records, Phoenix finds information about Mmuo, Saaed, and herself. With the introduction to Phoenix's mother figures, Okorafor once again rejects stereotypes about African American females. Harris documents the discriminatory and harmful caricatures created about African American women, noting that they tend to revolve around the body and what various shapes imply (8–9). Whereas larger bodies were characterized as the Mammy figure, as one who was asexual but ever-present and kind, thin women denoted a lack of caring ability (Harris 9). Harris also highlights the strength attribute inherent in literature about African American women. Here, the theorist writes about the African American woman as the protector, as "towers of strength" against violent forces, but, notably, Harris also sees this trait as harmful to the family (9–10). Harris observes that "Many readers and scholars—and even the other literary characters themselves—choose to ignore the problems inherent in the strength of these female characters in favor of highlighting the larger, sometimes positive, attributes of that strength" (10). While Harris is referring to adult literary characters, the same may be said about Okorafor's Phoenix. The protagonist may be a survivor, but at what cost? Throughout Okorafor's novel, Phoenix's joining a community, a family, is problematic. She has been conditioned to act as an individual because she has been forcefully separated from the other speciMEN and populace in New York. While in the tower, she spends her time alone in her room unless she is surrounded by the scientists, or she is in the cafeteria, in a room full of people where she must exist alone. The only person that she is close to is Saaed, and once her escape from enslavement may be successfully accomplished, she accepts the elusive Mmuo into her life. The issue is that in her efforts to destroy the Big Eye, she periodically overlooks her friends in favor of her mission.

While searching the Tower Records, Phoenix is overwhelmed by the nature of the information she encounters; as a result, she disregards the danger surrounding her and her companions while in the library. Both male characters are then physically required to remove Phoenix from the library before discovery, and it is not until she sees Mmuo at the restaurant, the space to where they escaped, that she awakens from her fixed state. By succumbing to her suffering and to her desire for vengeance, Phoenix somewhat rejects the superhuman stereotype. Throughout Okorafor's novel, Phoenix desires to undertake the destruction of the Big Eye but, on many occasions, she attempts to do so alone. When Phoenix shows that the records have affected her, she appears less than invincible—more like a human adolescent who is unsure of herself rather than an indestructible being. Harris continues her examination of the superhuman female construct by noting, "I define strong black women characters as sinning against their families and their communities when their motives are more self-absorbed and selfishly *individualistic*, in spite of claims to the contrary" (19). Here, Harris offers Dorothy West's Cleo Judson and her quest for increased social standing as one of her examples of the aforementioned (19). Phoenix becomes upset as she reads her friends' files while simultaneously consumed by her own pain. In fact, the character of Seven, who appears as both her father and her adviser, comments on Phoenix's state of being: "You are angrier than any woman I know" (Okorafor, *BP* ch. 18). He proceeds to educate Phoenix about her emotions and, notably, before this exchange occurs Seven questions her motivations, why she wishes to obliterate the towers and release the other speciMEN. Worryingly, it appears that Okorafor continues to perpetuate the angry Black woman stereotype at this moment in her novel. Previously, the winged man inquired as to Phoenix's intentions regarding the future. In reference to YA science fiction, Mendlesohn delineates what she terms the "romance novel," which she divides into two subcategories. *The Book of Phoenix* falls into the subcategory Mendlesohn describes as containing "two young people [who] are thrown together and 'inevitably' fall in love (sometimes with a heavy pinch of destiny)" (*Inter-Galactic* 123). It is disconcerting for the reader to observe that once Phoenix has a life-changing moment—she has sex with Saaed—she is no longer shown as an adolescent with numerous options for her future. Instead, her choices are limited to her being cast into one of two roles: stereotypical Black female savior or villain. The romantic relationship with Saaed appears forced and contrived; there does not appear to be any real need for Saaed in Phoenix's life other than his acting as catalyst for her escape from the tower. There are few males in her life—Saaed, Mmuo, and Seven—and Saaed appears as her love interest by default, as he is the closest to representing normality. Saaed is, after all, described by Phoenix in concrete terms: "Saaed was human. More human than I" (Okorafor, *BP* ch. 1). Phoenix's plans for the future do not include Saaed even though she professes to love him; Mendlesohn has stated in reference to young adult science fiction novels[1] that they tend to assert heteronormativity, which is what Okorafor's does. At the end of the novel, by having Phoenix and Saaed separate—he is the elderly man in Sunuteel's community that calls himself an Arab and teaches him English—Okorafor shows that Phoenix's future is one that she must live alone. It is in the conclusion that Okorafor moves away from the heteronormative "happily ever after," a point that will be examined later in the chapter. The other male who is almost always with Phoenix is Mmuo, the character with the ability to walk through solid objects and who spends the novel naked; due to his inability and lack of desire to conform to societal guidelines, he dies at the close of the text. Seven, the character who acts as her guide and father figure, makes the implication that Phoenix must utilize her emotions in a positive way, to be the leader of the freedom movement, or she will be consumed by her anger. Phoenix's community—love interest, friend, and father—has been included to offer her support in her transition from adolescent to adult but, unfortunately, her journey to the awareness of self is not a healthy one. As she is contemplating her life's direction, Phoenix seeks out her two mothers in her hope that they may be able to provide much needed background information.

While reading her Big Eye record, Phoenix notices a note in the file, one that references HeLa, thereby connecting her to Phoenix. Phoenix realizes that the two of them are linked, but it is unclear to Phoenix as to how. As Okorafor's novel is undoubtedly a neo-slave narrative, omitting the parentage for this character is not a deviation from the norm for this genre. Symbolically, making her the descendant of numerous African people enables them to have a voice through Phoenix. Before Phoenix ventures to Tower 4, Seven informs her that he will not be able to go with her, as his destiny lies in New York. When Phoenix questions his choice of locale, Seven informs her that New York requires his assistance more than Africa because while it has once again been wounded, it will heal in time. In a review of Okorafor's novel, Catherine Mann refers to the impact that the colonial Occident has on other spaces, specifically that it is "a critique of the big, powerful systems and structures that are part of Western culture. This is about marginalised and dispossessed people interacting with, or against, an authoritarian establishment which sees them only as resources. This includes comment on how the West interacts with other parts of the world and how organisations treat the people they exploit" (Mann). Okorafor highlights the body as a site of consumption, offering striking parallels between Phoenix's society and her own. Seven advises Phoenix that he is there to help her "because you are change, Phoenix. Wherever you go, you bring revolution" (Okorafor, *BP* ch. 18). Phoenix does speak to Seven about her parentage, namely asking him if he is, indeed, her father; when she searches the LifeGen files, she discovers her real parentage and asks, "How could I have no father? How could I be nothing but a cataclysm spurred by weapons engineers and scientists? I was nothing but the result of a slurry of African DNA and cells" (Okorafor, *BP* ch. 13). Here, Phoenix's adolescent experience is one that is expected of the norm. During her journey toward adulthood, Phoenix seeks knowledge about her background, her origins, in order to fully form her identity. Unfortunately, what Phoenix learns is that people of African origin are considered by much of the West to be disposable commodities. One of her mothers is Lucy, the character Okorafor terms the "mitochondrial Eve," the child/adult that provides her DNA to Phoenix and holds humanity's "genetic blueprint" within her. Like Phoenix, the Big Eye scientists abused her physical body and altered her so that she would not physically age: she remained ten years old until her suicide. Phoenix's other mother was her surrogate, Vera Takeisha Thomas, the woman that spends the remainder of her life after Phoenix's birth in a mental institution within a federal prison.

Vera is a representation of the voiceless just as Phoenix is a literal and physical representation of those who have been objectified. Harris, in reference to the slave mother figure in Toni Morrison's *Beloved*, states that "Baby Suggs locates the power to save one's self within the confines of one's body and the strength of one's mind, thereby denying to slaveholders the very structure, the very frame they have claimed as property" (Harris 62). As has been noted, it is consistent with the slave narrative structure that Phoenix is kept ignorant of her parentage; however, as this text is also YA she ventures forth on a journey of discovery, namely she goes to speak with Vera to discover more about her origins. Clare Bradford, in "Race, Ethnicity and Colonialism," documents the appearance of the Oompa-Loompas in Roald Dahl's *Charlie and the Chocolate Factory*, citing them as "a representation of a group of immigrant workers exploited by a factory owner" (39). When Phoenix locates Vera's record in the tower, she is dismayed to find that Vera wanted to retain custody of her but that because she was a surrogate—she is paid for the use of her body as a receptacle for Phoenix—the child was taken from her. Okorafor shows the "exploit[ation]" of Vera; the Big Eye uses the cisgendered woman's body as it sees fit no matter the cost (Bradford 39). According to Phoenix, it is having to give up her child (if biological imperative must be considered here, then it should be noted that Okorafor emphasizes Vera's ethnicity as African American, therefore there is a historical and cultural connection between the two) that pushes her toward mentally instability. Again, Okorafor channels the slave mother figure, specifically the impact that the theft of her child and, in many cases, the sale of the child has on her mental well-being. Turning toward one of the most significant neo-slave narratives, *Beloved*, Harris states that "Baby Suggs's laying on of hands . . . restores Baby Suggs to the role of strong and supportive mother that had been wrenched away from her during slavery" (60). The nurturing women washing Sethe's body appear in Okorafor's novel as Phoenix and her visit to the tower that confines Vera. As Phoenix delineates Vera's experience, she highlights the abuses by the Big Eye. When Vera offers to be a surrogate, she does so in the desire to be healed after the loss of her three children in a fire. The Big Eye takes advantage of her fragile mental state and uses her body without any consideration of what may transpire in the long run: Phoenix is a speciMEN and as such the risk to Vera from giving birth to one is high, a risk not mentioned to her.

When Phoenix locates Vera, first and foremost she focuses her attention on her space, the Triple Towers Correctional Facility in Los Angeles. Even though Vera has been promised great advantages upon delivering Phoenix (for example, a house, disease prevention, etc.), she spends the remainder of her life in a prison cell, a space meant to represent the slave's abode in the slave narrative. Phoenix tells her listener, "So they never gave her her own house, but they did force her into a home: D41 D-Pod Room Number 7" (Okorafor, *BP* ch. 21). Okorafor alludes to American historical reality, that enslaved people did not own property and that some who rebelled against the system were forced into mental institutions for doing so. As Phoenix enters the cell, she describes its state, which is one of squalor, and that of Vera. Notably, Okorafor clearly intends to connect the space and Vera, implying parallels between the two. Vera's body is like the space—it is now her prison. By giving birth to a speciMEN and subsequently having the child taken from her, Vera becomes physically and mentally incapacitated. When Phoenix walks from Vera's bathroom, she approaches her mother seated in a wheelchair and physically reveals herself to her. By removing her burka and grasping Vera's hands with her own, Phoenix makes herself vulnerable to Vera. When she looks at Vera, Phoenix tells her listener, "This was the woman who was willing to die for me. This was my mother" (Okorafor, *BP* ch. 21). The revelation of identity and the physical laying on of hands enact a healing for Vera, thereby enabling her to, if only briefly, have a voice. When she speaks she immediately calls Phoenix by name and asserts that it was she who named her upon her birth. Regarding her heritage, Phoenix's curiosity, a tenet of children's literature, leads to her search for Vera and Vera's subsequent redemption. In their conversation Vera reaffirms the importance of African culture—the naming ceremony—and that Western colonialism is continuing. To Phoenix, Vera offers a warning when she refers to the Big Eye as "Modern day slavers!" (Okorafor, *BP* ch. 21). As Phoenix and Vera converse, Phoenix obtains some information she needs to enact change in her society, to do as Seven has observed. Mendlesohn discusses the 1950s' children's science fiction literature series, Miss Pickerell, stating that "Science and the art of growing up is firmly anchored in the notion of listening and asking questions" (*Inter-Galactic* 85). During their talk, Vera is permitted for the first time since her contract with the Big Eye to make choices for herself. Phoenix questions Vera about her experiences while also attempting to rescue her from her imprisonment; Vera does not wish to leave with Phoenix but does want Phoenix to "Give 'em hell" and to choose the moment of her death (Okorafor, *BP* ch. 21). Vera dies in her daughter's arms once she has vocalized Big Eye's false promises (she asserts they promised she could retain custody of Phoenix) and for Phoenix to take control and, essentially, to abolish enslavement in her society. Trites discusses YA literature and the parent/child relationship: "Even if parent figures are absent from an adolescent novel, their physical absence often creates a psychological presence that is remarked upon as a sort of repression felt strongly by the adolescent character" (*Disturbing* 56). Her mother's death and revelation about the Big Eye act as a catalyst for Phoenix's transformation. She removes her burka and returns to Saaed and the Sandcastle Hotel, where the Big Eye attacks.

Here, Phoenix joins with her community to battle the Big Eye; however, Vera's words are not her only motivator. When she flies to the hotel, Phoenix discovers that Mmuo has died. She goes to his body on the beach and examines him, highlighting her belief that Mmuo was attempting to phase between objects when the Big Eye shot him. In an examination of the displaying of physically disabled bodies in America and Britain, specifically documenting the freak show, Thomson observes that both live and deceased bodies were placed on display for viewers. Noting that almost neither—the live or deceased body—carries more weight with the viewer than the other, as the value of the material lies in the significance of the body itself, the exploitation of the disabled figure, Thomson states that "If live exhibition was enhanced by animation and performance, the display of a dead prodigy embalmed as a spectacle, pickled as a specimen, or textualized as an anatomical drawing derived from dissection was equally profitable, and often more readable and manipulable" (57). On the beach, Phoenix witnesses Mmuo's corpse; symbolically, it is partially buried beneath the sand while the exposed section is cleansed by the incoming tide. It is not the sight of the dead children holding Mmuo's hand, children that Mmuo was presumably trying to save, that affects Phoenix but the death of her friend and comrade-in-arms. Mmuo is not only a member of her community but a representation of the power that the corporation has over others. Thomson continues, "Freaks and prodigies were solely bodies, without the humanity social structures confer upon more ordinary people" (57). To an onlooker, Mmuo's body would be as Thomson has noted; however, Phoenix is also a speciMEN. Because she is like Mmuo and exists in the category of Other, her reaction to seeing his body is one of emotion. Containing bullet holes, Mmuo's body may read as performative. The Big Eye wishes to continue to use Mmuo to serve its purpose and in this instance to instill fear in others. For Phoenix, the children's bodies are attempting to gain the attention, the caregiving that she craves. Commenting about the missing parental figure, Trites notes that "this absence then becomes, in turn, a presence against which the adolescent character rebels. When adolescent characters transform an absent character into a presence against which they can rebel, they are creating a parent who is present as *logos*, as Word, through which and against which to develop" (*Disturbing* 56). This scene offers the reader a glimpse of the childlike state of Phoenix. She is physically an adult, but mentally she has not completed this transition. She refuses to comply with the directions of Seven and Vera. Her community—one of the only fixed presences in her life—has died, and she no longer wishes to be the hero that saves the world. Instead, Phoenix desires to mourn for her friend and, for a moment in time, to be the only two people on that beach. For a brief period, Phoenix wants to be selfish and, therefore, normal. Phoenix's act of indignantly pushing away the children's bodies is not an unfeeling one; rather, she behaves as a young person unwilling to share the last moment with her family with anyone else.

Once Seven, Vera, and Mmuo die, the only person that remains in Phoenix's life is Saaed. In the discussion of the "substitute parent" in reference to Finn and Jim's relationship in Mark Twain's novel *Adventures of Huckleberry Finn*, Trites says that "as with an actual parent, Huck must rebel against this *in loco parentis* figure before he can grow" (*Disturbing* 60). With regard to Phoenix, the reader must ask, does Phoenix mature? As her community dies, Phoenix becomes more resentful and irate, even territorial. She witnesses the Big Eye attacking Saaed, "my Saaed," and begins to burn. She only leaves the scene once Saaed reminds her that he is immortal and tells her to depart and save herself (Okorafor, *BP* ch. 23). Phoenix alternates between "I could kill them all. Make them all ash" and acting as Saaed wishes she would (Okorafor, *BP* ch. 23). She saves herself, and in the name of rebellion, but clearly also revenge, Phoenix burns the world. In the chapter titled "Who Fears the Reaper," Phoenix documents her desire to abolish enslavement but also to institute a "military strategy called 'scorched earth'" (*BP* ch. 24). She rejects other gods, embracing Ani, thereby calling herself "Ani's soldier" (*BP*). While ultimately Phoenix complies with the wishes of her parental figures and her family—Seven, Vera, even Mmuo—she takes it to extremes, becoming a zealot. Trites observes that when analyzing literature directed toward an adolescent audience, one must be mindful of the message that is being sent. Momentarily, it appears that Phoenix is comparing herself to early twentieth-century superheroes, but then she asserts that she acts in accordance with Ani's "will. Ani has asked me to wipe the slate clean" (Okorafor, *BP* ch. 24). Phoenix takes it upon herself to be the hand of God and enact a violent cleansing of the Earth, symbolically starting with New York. When the story finishes, Sunuteel is afraid, especially when Phoenix speaks to him through his portable, telling him not to alter her story. Both Sunuteel and his wife take measures to tell Phoenix's story, but, disturbingly, Sunuteel believes that Phoenix is a god.

Like in *The Book of Phoenix*, *Binti* revolves around an adolescent female protagonist, one that also has unusual gifts that lead her to transform her societal construct. Okorafor's newest series, *Binti*, also concentrates on the metamorphosis of the adolescent female. In fact, Okorafor has said that she wrote the first novella in this series when faced with a life-changing decision of her own: when she left Chicago to take the position of professor at the University of Buffalo. As Okorafor has verbally asserted in numerous venues, she relates to Farai Chideya, an interviewer for NPR, how she went about creating the first Binti novella. In both her conversation with Chideya and her talk to the Science Fiction Research Association in June 2017, Okorafor revealed her desire to accept the professorship, but that she was apprehensive about leaving her home and family and so were they. Like Okorafor, Binti "had to just go" ("Hugo"); she needed to leave Earth and take the spaceship off-world to Oomza University. Ultimately, Okorafor's novella revolves around the adventure and Binti's "trajectory of socialization" (Mendlesohn 87). In the fourth chapter of *The Inter-Galactic Playground: A Critical Study of Children's and Teens' Science Fiction*, Mendlesohn examines the development of the adolescent science fiction adventure story from the 1950s to the first decade of the twenty-first century. Mendlesohn documents that the 1950s' YA novel concentrates on a plot where an adolescent is directed toward a future career, whereas late 1960s' and 1970s' works focus on an adolescent rebellion against parents and their societal choices. Here, attempting to find one's own way in life is integral to the development of the adolescent character, but it should be noted, that "adults and their values are still very much the center and focus of children's and teens' ambitions" (Mendlesohn 87). Significantly, once the twenty-first century is reached, Mendlesohn asserts that the parental figure is still present in the adolescent's life but that if the adolescent's path in life no longer corresponds with that of the adult, this character renounces the parent's societal direction (93).

When Okorafor's novella begins, Binti is rushing to leave for the university, her haste predicated on her refusal to remain on Earth as her culture dictates. Her rebellion begins with her use of technology, the transporter, to get her to the shuttle. Even though the Himba do utilize some technology, they are not reliant on it, preferring instead the ways of the past and those with a connection to the soil. As with *Phoenix*, technology is portrayed as deceptive, problematic if it is prioritized over one's culture. Binti describes the transporter as inexpensive and on the verge of breaking down; she wills it to work, as the alternative is a lengthy walk to the shuttle. Notably, as the transporter starts, Binti touches the otjize on her skin and then the ground, verbally offering her gratitude to the land for supporting her desire to go to the university. Binti reveals her appreciation before she asserts the shame that her family is going to feel when they discover that she has left Earth. While imagining what may occur once her absence is noted, she pictures her aunts and uncles discussing "how I'd scandalized our entire bloodline. I was going to be a pariah" (*Binti*). Here, the issue is not only that Binti, in true adolescent fashion, sneaks out of her house in the middle of the night but also that she refuses to follow the guidelines of her society and remain in their community on the planet. For Binti, it is not that she is reluctant to integrate her Himba culture as part of her life, it is that she refuses to follow their isolationist protocol. As she thinks about her family's shame, she loses her composure; in frustration, Binti thumps the transporter with her foot and repeatedly orders it to move. As Binti is attempting to flee, she is desirous of silence but accepts the loud sounds that her Himba ankle bracelets make. As noted previously, the traditional slave narrative begins with the statement regarding birth. For Binti, her birth has already occurred; she is an adolescent on a journey to adulthood at the start of the novella. I identify *Binti* as a neo-slave narrative partially due to the underlying discriminatory aspects in Okorafor's work. The protagonist is not being "deliberately malicious," one attribute in early twenty-first-century YA science fiction, when she departs her home but, instead, Binti must find her own way in life even if it means leaving her family and her community behind (*Inter-Galactic* 93). She departs the Himba homeland in an attempt to undergo a journey of maturation—an adventure that changes her, hopefully for the better. Analyzing the YA science fiction adventure story, Mendlesohn notes the alterations made to the plot for this age bracket, in particular the desire to remain in the domestic sphere for the early twenty-first-century YA protagonist.[2]

In her chapter, "Paradox of Authority," Trites discusses first- and third-person narration, noting that the latter narrator may have "access to more power" than the former due to its inherent access to information (71). Interestingly, and Trites references the 1970s' first-person confessional narrators here, in particular that of S. E. Hinton (i.e., Mark in *That Was Then, This Is Now*), there is the possibility that "the narrator can be thought of as having power over readers because he is transmitting to them information that they may not have previously had" (Trites 71). When dealing with a slave narrative, as has been previously discussed in this chapter, it must be noted that the formerly enslaved person tells the story, thereby controlling the method in which content is transmitted to the reader. The control had by the formerly enslaved person is somewhat negated by the presence of the authenticating documents placed before and after the narrative itself. The formerly enslaved person's power over their story and formation of identity is no longer in the hands of the formerly enslaved person, but others; this is even more apparent when the formerly enslaved person does not have literacy skills and has dictated their narrative to someone, usually an abolitionist, to write down. Kristi McDuffe acknowledges that in early twenty-first-century texts, there is a fear of adolescents lacking literacy, which is portrayed in numerous instances as a reliance on technology (145). When Binti's story begins, once again Okorafor has elected to utilize first-person narration; it is Binti that appears in control of the story, as it is her voice that the reader witnesses, but the emotions that are exposed denote a lack of narrational control. Unfortunately, Binti is not desirous of an education because she wishes to obtain knowledge; rather she is more concerned with finding a space in which she fits in.

In keeping with Mendlesohn's outline of the YA science fiction adventure story, Binti's story revolves around her yearning to go to and subsequent attendance at school, specifically one that is housed away from her community. Mendlesohn thoughtfully provides a list of early twenty-first-century science fiction novels that concentrate on a "protagonist [that] actually leaves home and has scary adventures," indicating that during this time period the age of the main character may fluctuate but that these texts are aimed at a significantly younger audience than previous decades (98). Those written for "mid to late teens" contain a plotline in which the protagonist's story unfolds in the domestic sphere: many occur in a school, and "when protagonists do go on the run, it is with their parents" (Mendlesohn 98). Clearly, the writers of these novels are internalizing and subsequently displaying the phenomenon of millennials remaining with parents for much longer than has been witnessed previously. The reader must be mindful when examining Okorafor's novella, in which Binti physically separates herself from her parents, that in a slave narrative the enslaved person often escapes for nonslaveholding spaces alone. This is a journey that the formerly enslaved person is required to take individually, without any family. As is integral to the slave narrative, the former slave never cuts ties with their culture; in fact, ideology remains with the former slave, grounding his or her identity. Binti asserts, "I was never going to have a normal life, really" (Okorafor *Binti*). According to the protagonist, her exceptionally high scores on the planetary examination in math, while highlighting her intelligence and proficiency in this area, have caused great difficulty in her life. By taking this test, Binti receives official confirmation that she is different and it offers her an excuse to leave; she feels that she is not capable of conforming to societal guidelines, so she arranges to continue her psychological development—she attends university. As

Mendlesohn observes, the protagonist continues to have a connection to the domestic space: "The trajectory seems to be to go out in the world, learn something about the universe, and use this to have a reconciliation with the parental or familial unit" (102). On her way to the university, the ship is invaded by the Meduse, a species at war with the Khoush. As the students and staff are decimated by the Meduse, Binti, through the use of her technology and her people's ability as harmonizers, makes contact with the Meduse and subsequently brokers peace between the two cultures. After earning acceptance at the university, Binti returns home in the sequel, *Binti: Home*, where she endeavors to garner further acceptance, this time from her family and her community. As with the slave narrative, Binti voices her journey, in which the obtainment of education features prominently.

In summation, Okorafor utilizes the neo-slave narrative under the guise of the YA dystopic text. Throughout her recorded narrative, Phoenix metaphorically builds herself a body through which her story is told. She refuses to allow the Big Eye corporation to enslave her, to possess her physically or mentally. Each time she burns hot enough that she turns to ash and is subsequently physically reborn, she enters into a new phase of her maturation until she ultimately reaches a mental age that corresponds with the age of her physical body. Unfortunately, Okorafor takes her protagonist's progress too far, so that instead of resembling an adolescent reaching adulthood, the novel closes with Phoenix portrayed as a godlike figure. In Genesis, the Christian god cleanses Earth with the great flood of water but saves Noah, his family, and the animals. The Fan people from West Africa have a similar myth about the orishas that cleanse the Earth using fire; by doing so they try to ridthe world of Fam, a human that they created in their image. Fam abused his power and refuses to worship the gods; once the cleansing was complete the gods create Sekume, their additional attempt at making humanity, although this time man is mortal. Okorafor follows these mythological models as well as the slave narrative when she creates Phoenix's story. Like the Fan gods, Phoenix utilizes her abilities to rid her society of those that abuse their power; subsequently, she leaves behind the recording—her narrative—as a warning to the next generation. Like Phoenix, Binti's learned knowledge offers awareness, but, unfortunately for the protagonist, it is of individuality. Binti discovers she is different from her community; with her mathematical skills come those that make her a harmonizer. This ability makes her desirable to her family because it means she can take over the family business as a maker of astrolabes. It also ensures that she will complete her university application in secret, and, henceforth, she is thrust into an unsheltered society. Once she leaves her community, she is subjected to constant scrutiny. From the Khoush women in the airport dissecting her appearance to the male student, Heru, who touches her hair plaits without her permission, Binti is objectified for her difference. Before she leaves home, her mother asserts that the university will use her and refers to it as enslavement. As her astrolabe is scanned at the airport and her life revealed, the airport representative informs her, "You are the pride of your people, child" (Okorafor *Binti*). It is Binti's connection to her community and her individuality that allow for her bond with the Meduse, the end to the war, and her survival. Both Phoenix and Binti undergo a transformation that ultimately permits freedom for more than just themselves.

AFROHORROR AND THE GENDERED NARRATOR

Progression and Regression of the Adolescent Female Activist Character in the Devil's Wake Series and the Parables Series

INTRODUCTION

Husband and wife team, Steven Barnes and Tananarive Due, paired to write a dystopic young adult series revolving around female and male adolescent protagonists. In the initial novel in the Devil's Wake series (2012) of the same name, the text alternates narrators, with the female protagonist, Kendra, starting the novel. The alternating narrator—female and male—is a recognizable constructive pattern within adolescent literature, one that leads to differing perspectives of the plot that unfolds for the reader. Unfortunately, there are occasions in young adult literature where these points of view are stereotypically gendered, thereby offering readers inappropriate glimpses into what is supposed to be a representation of twenty-first-century American society as seen through the eyes of an adolescent. For this chapter, the gendered behavior of the female protagonist, Kendra Brookings, in the Devil's Wake series will be investigated. Further, the conspicuous parallels to Octavia E. Butler's Parables series is examined, particularly centering on the constructed utopic space. Since the monograph overall primarily concentrates on the neo-slave narrative genre, and since it is the experiences of African Americans that are researched here, readers must be mindful that not all scholarship that examines young adult media contributions applies to this study. While much of YA scholarship centers on adolescents who are engaged in a collective experience, writers take on the point of view that all adolescents' experiences are the same. Academic writers more often than not, even in the twenty-first century, do not take into account that the lives of many Black adolescents have been impacted by discrimination and collective trauma due to the lasting effects of enslavement. Even during the second wave of Black Lives Matter, scholarship about young adult texts featuring Black characters was still uncommon; it is this imbalance that this monograph attempts to rectify.

HOW BLACK CHARACTERS ARE REFLECTED IN SCHOLARSHIP AND IN LITERARY OUTPUTS

As previously observed, it is integral to the study of young adult literature that researchers examine texts as a young adult reader rather than an adult academic; this fact has been documented frequently by scholars. Readers must remember that young adult texts are not meant for them but an adolescent readership, one who is continuously influenced by the adult society in which they are immersed. While some writers have made an active attempt to offer literary outputs that reflect their diverse readership and the susceptibility of their readers, others bypass the need for diversity and inclusion entirely. For example, Naomi Kritzer's *Catfishing on CatNet* (2019) is an exceptional example of inclusion due to her emphasis on LGBTQ2S adolescents. Not only has Kritzer seamlessly utilized the nonbinary pronoun in her novel, she has also identified challenges facing women that live in fear of their abusers and the discrimination that biracial people face. In her first novel, one that was nominated for a Nebula Award, Kritzer demonstrates that authors do not need to browbeat their readers into acceptance of characters that are not cismale, heterosexual, and Caucasian. Her characters are brilliant in their strength yet are realistic, as they are not idealist portrayals. Ultimately, Kritzer's novel offers adolescent and adult readers alike positive cisgender young women and nonbinary young persons, never once feeling like an act of tokenism. A diverse and inclusive selection of literature like Kritzer's has been a long time coming, as has her recognition by a known body like the Nebula.

K. Ancrum's *The Weight of the Stars* is a novel made for twenty-first-century young adult and adult readers alike due to its emphasis on inclusivity and diversity. Utilizing postmodern constructivism—the novel is divided up into moments in time—Ancrum creates Ryann Byrd, a tall and muscular young woman with red hair whose parents die, leaving Ryann, her brother James, and his son Charlie, alone; they are frequently shown in their trailer in bed at night with the baby between them as they cling to one another for comfort. Ryann appears as having both physical and mental strength; however, it is the former that get her in trouble more than once. Ancrum crafts a diverse and inclusive group of friends for Ryann, adolescents that she has saved from loneliness and even from themselves. The story unfolds around "the new girl's" presence in school; Alexandria, the biracial daughter of an adolescent astronaut pushes everyone away, only desirous of spending time on her roof hoping to receive messages from her mother in space. Over the course of the novel, Ryann and Alexandria grow closer, pledging forever love when Ryann goes to space. On her site, Ancrum guarantees diversity and inclusion in her writing, even offering viewers a list for their perusal. Ancrum, who identifies as a bi, intersex African American writer, creates a wonderfully supportive friend group for Ryann and Alexandria, including Ahmed, a child of a three-partner marriage; Shannon, the popular one of the group, whose brother had to leave her religiously strict household in order to pursue his dreams of the theater; and wealthy Tomas, who almost overdosed but for Ryann, who saves his life. Over time, each character becomes not only self-aware but communal-aware, caring and protecting others as well as themselves.

While Ancrum's novel fronts inclusion, it is problematic that both of her lesbian characters—Ryann and Alexandria—are physically cast into stereotypical body types.[1] Ryann is "butch," or coded masculine, while Alexandria's body is petite, or coded feminine. Also, there is concern because it is the middle-class biracial young woman that stays behind, as the low-income White-coded character[2] has her dreams fulfilled and goes to space. Ancrum's message is significant: on one hand, the financially disadvantaged yet caring Ryann becomes an astronaut, showing that low-income persons can complete the tasks that a financially advantaged person like Alexandria can. On the other hand, the biracial character does not go to space until many years later, and the low-income character only goes because Alexandria gives Ryann her place. Although Ancrum's novel contains some positive points for adolescent readers, the benefits are convoluted by the typecasting.

It was not until the 1970s that African American women writers' works were recognized for having literary value, proof that discrimination does exist in publishing as well as in academia and for readers. As previously mentioned, this monograph came to be due to the lack of attention paid to young adult publications featuring Black characters and those written by Black writers. Dystopian novels, novellas, and short stories written by and about the aforementioned were in short supply; therefore, what existed was critical to study. The challenge then becomes one of scrutiny. Ultimately (and there are many more selections in the late second and early third decades of the twenty-first century), the significance of these works should be brought to light but also should some questionable choices made by the writers, especially in the case of Barnes and Due's series. In effect, just because a selection of literature has been written by an African American writer, it does not make it good or appropriate for an adolescent reader.

There is a plethora of literature available from Caucasian writers about adolescents. Academics tend to concentrate on these texts in their examinations. In some cases, it is because the academic can relate because the writer is White, or is part of the LGBTQ2S community, or belongs to the working class (lived experiences). Sometimes, however, it is because these are the texts that become popular and are readily available or are heralded by publishers. On the one hand, these texts should not be ignored, while, on the other hand, being written by a Caucasian writer does not mean that the text is necessarily good. Texts that concentrate on the Black experience should not be ignored in favor of literature by and about White persons; however, just because a text contains the Black experience does not make it an accurate representation of Black experiences or one that is well written, as in the case of Barnes and Due's series.

Their initial novel in the two-book series begins with the voice of the female protagonist, Kendra. Kendra, a biracial introvert, relies heavily on her parents for guidance and has difficulty completing tasks without assistance. As Trites has well documented, children's literature tends to concentrate on the formation of individuality, while the young adult text has the adolescent character deconstructing the adult's societal makeup. As a sixteen-year-old only child, Kendra demonstrates that she has a desire to rebel but is uncertain about doing so. The narrator of *Devil's Wake* (*DW*) calls attention to Kendra's appearance: "Kendra herself looked too much like a typical Disney Channel Sassy Black Teenager for her own comfort: short, cute, chipmunk cheeks, perfect teeth, and eyes as bright as stars" (Barnes and Due *DW*, ch. 1). While the idyllic nature of Kendra's middle-class, suburban life may seem refreshing, Barnes and Due's saccharine Kendra rings false for a twenty-first-century novel meant for an adolescent audience. The standard literary construction regarding African American people is to offer characters that have been traumatized by their past racialized history, including a collective history of enslavement, of past American discriminatory practices, and of subsequent trauma. There are Black voices that have asserted a desire to venture away from literary plots that only document these experiences (see Scott Woods referenced later in this chapter) as there is a tendency in academia and publishing to confine African American writers and characters to this track. Fundamentally, there is also the tendency, as initiated by the Harlem Renaissance and W. E. B. Du Bois, to idealize the experiences of African Americans in order to show African Americans as upwardly mobile. For a twenty-first-century audience, an idealized characterization of an adolescent or her lifestyle does not ring true to a postmodern readership, adolescent and adult alike. In a century continuously tainted by discriminatory practices toward Black persons as well as wars, 9/11, and environmental disasters, offering a teenager who has-it-all is unrealistic, and they cannot emotionally connect with the audience.

When there is a violent attack at the hospital where she is to receive a flu shot, Kendra is physically unable to flee. Her parents must bodily remove her from the vicinity; once her parents die, Kendra, a traumatized adolescent, withdraws into her writing. This behavior makes it glaringly obvious that Barnes and Due have capitalized on the "special snowflake" adolescent construct. Kendra is physically and mentally incapacitated when confronted with challenges. Once Kendra loses her parents, she initially goes to live with Grandpa Joe, a Vietnam veteran who teaches her how to survive on her own and how to utilize nature in order to do so. Once he dies, she joins a new community and heads toward Devil's Wake island and later Domino Falls in the novel of the same name, both of which are purported to be utopic refuges in California.

THE RESEMBLANCE TO OCTAVIA E. BUTLER'S *PARABLE OF THE SOWER*

If this plot seems oddly familiar, that is because it is. In the late twentieth century, Butler, the Queen of Afrofuturism, wrote the two-novel Parables series. In the first release, *Parable of the Sower* (*PS*; 1993), Lauren Oya Olamina is introduced and shown as part of a community existing on the fringes of Los Angeles. Lauren resides in a gated community until it is overrun by drug addicts desirous of societal chaos. Unlike Kendra who lives in a bubble, Lauren understands that the safety inside of Robledo is tenuous, that her father is demanding and overprotective because death continuously looms outside the border wall. Once life outside of the community invades, Lauren is thrown alone into the outside world, where she must form a new community so that she may survive. In both Barnes and Due's *DW* and Butler's *PS*, the female protagonists write in a diary, documenting their experiences for a future generation. Both protagonists also have a medical condition, making them hyperempathetic to others. After their respective families are lost, the young women wander the West Coast, seeking a new utopic space. One glaring difference between the series concerns that of the utopic space: while Lauren establishes Acorn, an intentional community that is successful until outside forces interfere, Domino Falls offers no safety—it is a cult and therefore is a false utopia. These spaces are supposed to be symbols of hope that humanity has the capacity to survive an event of apocalyptic proportions; however, only Butler excels at creating a utopic space complete with the Earthseed ideology—its own religious teachings based on the ancient premise that communal harmony aids in survival.

GENDERED CONSTRUCTS REGARDING AFRICAN AMERICAN WOMEN

Referencing the introduction of enslavement to America, bell hooks, in *Ain't I a Woman: Black Women and Feminism*, asserts that "Sexism was an integral part of the social and political order White colonizers brought with them from their European homelands, and it was to have a grave impact on the fate of enslaved black women" (15). Her text and its title acts as an homage to Sojourner Truth's address to the 1851 Women's Rights Convention in Akron, Ohio, where the formerly enslaved Truth documented the treatment of African American females, and the meaning of this is twofold. First, hooks and Truth record the oppressive treatment of African American women during enslavement, asserting its continuous misogynist and racist aftereffects. This includes the stereotypes (Mammy, Sapphire, and Jezebel constructs) and their subsequent perpetuation, which were constructed to restrain Black women's sense of selves and their physical societal movement.

Additionally, with regard to hooks and Truth, their respective statements make reference to Zora Neale Hurston's famed statement about African American women. It is the African American woman who Hurston calls "de mule uh de world,"[3] the woman upon whom all burdens rest. If examining Barnes and Due's series and that of Butler as neo-slave narratives, the aforementioned assertions from these three brilliant women should showcase the changing constructs of literary adolescent African American female protagonists—at least in Butler's case. Whereas Kendra's character is composed of stereotypical female attributes—she is almost mute, fearful, and submissive—Lauren is consistently portrayed as having great strength and the ability to lead. The librarian Scott Woods in his article, "28 More Black Picture Books That Aren't about Boycotts, Buses or Basketball" (2018), offers his guidelines for choosing books to review and what the writer should call attention to in the review: "Shine light on typically ignored aspects of black life. Nothing against history, but we aren't exactly hurting for books on slavery. We *could* do with some more books about fishing, owning pets, and generally any other hobby children have." Marlene S. Barr, in her analysis of science fiction featuring Black children, forwards that "Realistic black canonical literature, after all, is as depressing as realistic feminist canonical literature" (85). Woods's and Barr's observations are problematic; writers and audiences may not ignore the history of discrimination (and may not want to do so) in favor of a sanitized reality. When examining the series, both females become leaders of their respective communities; however, while Lauren offers guidance through her mental acuity, Kendra is the "heart" of hers, thereby typecasting her as both the emotional female stereotype and reinforcing the African American stereotype of the female as caregiver. Woods does offer an attempt at normalized imagery associated with people of color in an effort to reclaim African American literature from being typecasted as only about the antebellum South. As an example, *Doc McStuffins* may be offered as a mainstream popular cultural contribution that appears to place the historical past in the background while embracing for all children an African American female child who aspires to be like her mother—a doctor. Brooks Barnes, writing for the *New York Times*, documents that Disney has attracted more African American viewers due to the series, which is saying something, as this same company released *Song of the South*. The *Doc McStuffins* children's television series presents young viewers realism and positivism simultaneously, thereby enacting the message of the Afrofuturist genre. Ultimately, Butler and her contemporaries dispense justice for past wrongs as they positively place African Americans at the forefront of the future. Within the slave narrative, neo-slave narrative, and the Afrofuturist text, the utopic space is sought as a refuge from invading outside forces, usually representative of racist societal behavior.

UTOPIAS, DYSTOPIAS, AND AFROFUTURISM: AFRICAN AMERICAN FUTURES AND THE HAPPY ENDING

When analyzing a slave narrative, the reader must consistently take into account that the most coveted piece of information within the text is the escape. It is this moment, the climax of the literary contribution, that the abolitionist or would-be abolitionist audience has been awaiting because it imparts to the reader how the enslaved person journeyed to safety in the North. As Melvin Dixon demonstrates in his essay "Singing Swords: The Literary Legacy of Slavery," which documents textual forms originating from slavery, the slave narrative was widely read after 1840 (299). In reference to the slave narrative and the songs created by the enslaved, Dixon states that "Both forms of cultural expression from the slave community create a vision of history, an assessment of the human condition, and a heroic fugitive character unlike any other in American literature" (298). It is this figure and their quest for freedom that Butler and Barnes and Due have attempted to emulate with their novels. Dixon's observation that ultimately the slave narratives contain "ideologies for survival" is consistent with the material presented in the neo-slave narratives (300). The idyllic myth presented within the slave narratives is consistent with the characterization of the enslaved person as a "heroic fugitive." In order for the slave narrative to be effective, thereby reaching its socially distanced northern reader, the formerly enslaved person must be shown as one of the lucky ones who reaches Eden. Essentially, what the reader encounters is a fairy tale ending of sorts, a glossed over version of events to come once the newly free slave immerses themselves in northern society. It is this surface-level representation of the North that the neo-slave narrative endeavors to remedy. In effect, the North is a utopic representation, a constructed space that represents hope for those enslaved in the South, but as many Black persons discovered during the Great Migration, the North was more dystopian than utopian.

For this analysis, it is necessary to differentiate between the utopic and dystopic spaces, as both make appearances in slave narratives and neo-slave narratives. Utopian theorist Lyman Tower Sargent differentiates between a utopic and dystopic space: "If viewed with hope, the result is usually a utopia. If viewed with alarm, the result is usually a dystopia" (Introduction, *Utopianism*). Further, in his article "The Three Faces of Utopianism Revisited," Sargent defines a dystopia as "a non-existent society described in considerable detail and normally located in time and space that the author intended a contemporaneous reader to view as considerably worse than the society in which that reader lived" (9). Raffaella Baccolini and Tom Moylan, editors of *Dark Horizons: Science Fiction and the Dystopian Imagination*, outline the changes made to the construction of the literary utopic space throughout the twentieth century. In their introduction, the experts in utopic studies observe that after the early 1980s cyberpunk meditation on commodification came "several sf writers [that] confronted the decade's simultaneous silencing and cooptation of Utopia by turning to dystopian strategies as a way to come to terms with the changing social reality" ("Introduction"). Butler is one such writer and, tellingly, her name is offered in a list of female writers. While this sampling positively reflects the number of women writers in this field, it also shows how few African American women were recognized at the turn of the century. Even after the second wave of Black Lives Matter, which emphasized the lack of Black persons in varied fields, Butler tends to be named in lists comprising either science fiction women writers or African American writers; she tends to be celebrated as a niche writer instead of a MacArthur Grant–winning artist. Maria Varsam is one of few writers that have identified Butler's *Parable of the Sower* as containing a society based on enslavement. Varsam incorporates Butler's novel in a collection of literature including George Orwell's *Nineteen Eighty-Four*; however, she sets Butler's novel apart from those that include authoritarian spaces because of its addition of "debt slavery" (Varsam). Conclusively, Varsam's is not an examination of raced enslavement: "The concerns of dystopian fiction often coincide with those of slave narratives in their discourse on freedom, inequality, and the nature of domination." The study contained within this chapter favors the usage of intersectionality, as ethnicity cannot be separated from identity or experience. If the reader follows the trajectory of both Barnes and Due's initial novel and that of Butler, stages from the plot identical to that from the slave narrative are clearly visible. So that a text may be considered a neo-slave narrative, the plot must have more than a faint resemblance to the slave narrative's path from slavery to freedom.

In examining Barnes and Due's series, it becomes apparent that their duo of novels does not satisfactorily fit within the genre of Afrofuturism due to its inclusion of the horror elements. De Witt

Douglas Kilgore expands on Dery's definition of Afrofuturism from "Black to the Future":

> Afrofuturist writers and scholars organize their work around at least three basic assumptions: that peoples of African descent, their ways and histories, will not disappear in any credible future; that the future, indeed, will be one in which the peoples of the African diaspora operate as the directors and beneficiaries of technological progress; and that the cultural meaning of blackness will continually change as generations advance. (569)

When examining both *DW* and *PS*, the reader may identify Moylan's notion that the

> dystopian narrative is largely the product of the terrors of the twentieth century. A hundred years of exploitation, repression, state violence, war, genocide, disease, famine, ecocide, depression, debt, and the steady depletion of humanity through the buying and selling of everyday life provided more than enough fertile ground for this fictive underside of the utopian imagination. (*Scraps* xi)

Moylan identifies the motif of fear within literature, one that plays a prominent role in both young adult science fiction and horror. It is in the latter subgenre where Barnes and Due's duo may be placed.

Young adult literature and film theorist Catherine Driscoll has thoroughly documented the conventions of the literary and cinematic genres involving adolescent girls. Analyzing adolescent films and adolescent horror, Driscoll identifies the mark of the horror film, namely the absence of knowledge. According to Driscoll (and other horror theorists including Bruce Kawin), "Horror must operate on the border between what we know and what we don't or, in fact, what can never be known" (83). When utilizing Butler's *PS* as a source text, Barnes and Due swapped Butler's raving, violent drug addicts for zombies, thereby making their duology adolescent horror. While the literary and cinematic horror offerings differ with respect to medium, it may be asserted that there are commonalities between the two. Conclusively, Barnes and Due's Devil's Wake series harbors many of the adolescent horror films' characteristics that Driscoll lays out in her argument about stereotypes and the repetitiveness of adolescent horror films. From the virgin protagonist character construct (Kendra) to that of the final girl, Barnes and Due manage to capture the most trite aspects of horror without adding any of the benefits of the genre. In his detailed analysis of horror in his text *Horror and the Horror Film*, Bruce Kawin contemplates theorists' explorations of the rationality behind moviegoers' intense admiration for the horror genre. Kawin sums up the interest in horror, offering, "The horror film provides a way to conceptualize, give a shape to and deal with the evil and frightening" (3). Horror offers readers and viewers the opportunity to have the Aristotelian cathartic experience while also learning about themselves and others. Due to the incorporation of the horror tropes as well as the appearance of Black characters in the future and the significance of the accumulation of knowledge, Barnes and Due's Devil's Wake series clearly belongs to the young adult Afrohorror subgenre. Furthering his description of horror, Kawin (as does Driscoll) analyzes the differing fears that alight in the genre; interestingly, Kawin detects that while horror reflects fears that are common among people, some are inherent to a specific cultural group (3). To readers of the young adult Afrohorror subgenre, the question must be posed even though it is uncomfortable: what is it that Black adolescent characters fear? In the Devil's Wake series, what do the zombies represent? For her Parables series, Butler begins *PS* highlighting not only societal fear regarding the aftereffects of a societal downturn but also the concerns (or lack thereof) that women have when taking medication while pregnant.

KNOWLEDGE FOR THE ENSLAVED: BIRTHDAYS AND WRITINGS

As is traditional within the slave narrative, the literacy of the enslaved person is key to the understanding of mental enslavement. When Sophia Auld relinquishes Douglass's education, he asserts that her actions have come too late, that he has already come to the understanding as to how enslavers were able to oppress the enslaved. Douglass describes how Sophia alters over time due to the influence of the institution of enslavement; here, Douglass refers to her withholding of knowledge from him as "mental darkness" (Douglass, ch. 6). Not only does Butler retain the traditional slave narrative structure—the birth statement, the accumulation of knowledge (i.e., education), and the escape—she concludes *PS* on a hopeful note, with the protagonist reaching the utopic space. Butler takes control of her fictional narrative, and rather than ending her work upon reaching the northern representational model, Lauren takes control of the space and founds an inclusive community. Butler's novel duo emphasizes the tropes of hope and survival linked to the accumulation of knowledge as duplicated in the neo-slave narrative. Ultimately, Butler's duo of novels is grounded in the Afrofuturism genre, the science fictional influence clear in the presentation of information to the reader.

Butler's novel opens with one of the passages from Lauren's Earthseed religion, asserting specifically the survivability of humanity. While it appears that Lauren's passage is to be comforting for the reader, one must question why it must be offered. Numerous YA theorists have observed that adolescent readers of science fiction tend to immerse themselves in literary contributions written for an adolescent audience and that for adults. C. W. Sullivan examines the initial publication in the young adult science fiction field, Robert A. Heinlein's *Rocket Ship Galileo* (1947), citing that the immense popularity of Heinlein's "juveniles" upon release was because he wrote about "the maturing of the human race as it spreads outward into the universe" (22). As Lauren's first chapter begins, under the notation that her diary entry is part of the official Earthseed doctrine, Lauren writes that Saturday July 20, 2024, is her fifteenth birthday; it is also her father's fifty-fifth. For Lauren, the adolescent protagonist, the birthday is a milestone in her life, and it is no accident that Butler elected to offer two birthdays that include the number five. According to Ian Stewart, this digit "symbolizes human life" and was also "often considered ... rebellious" (Stewart). There is an undercurrent of hopefulness when the novel begins that Lauren's Earthseed will enable humanity's survival off-world. Beginning with a birthday, a symbol of a fresh start for a new year, Lauren's tone is anticipatory of things to come; unfortunately, there is a despondency in her presentation. As Henry Louis Gates, Jr. observes in reference to the slave narrative, "In literacy lay the true freedom for the black slave," as "the slave who learned to read and write was the first to run away" ("Introduction" 1). Due to her method of transmission, Butler's *PS* may be considered a neo-slave narrative; Butler's accomplishment with this novel is not surprising, as it is she who wrote one of the earliest and most quintessential contributions to this genre—*Kindred*.

As previously asserted, Butler begins with a variation of one of the markers of the slave narrative according to Olney, the "I was born" statement. This beginning serves as an indicator that the enslaved person's existence is a reality even though pre-Civil War society refused to acknowledge its authenticity. Olney discusses the narrative content, stating that in order "to give a true picture of slavery as it really is, he [the enslaved] must maintain that he exercises a clear-glass, neutral memory that is neither creative nor faulty" (150). The formerly enslaved person's account of their life must be accurate and complete. If at any time Douglass was unable or unwilling to give factual knowledge to his readership, he had to offer his reasoning for doing so, or fear his account will be thought untrue. Due to the misnomer, her gender, and the omission of other enslaved people's stories, Harriet Jacobs's narrative has been placed in doubt since publication. Olney furthers his investigation into the presentation of the narrative, stating that the present and the past for the former enslaved person cannot intersect else the narrative may not be believable for the reader (151). Butler's Afrofuturist novel presents Lauren's past not only as a narrative but also as a religious text, one that contains the historical background of Earthseed's founder and validation for its inception. For Lauren in a postapocalyptic society where the government has fallen, there is no official record of her birth, so she creates the Earthseed diaries, thereby self-legitimizing her existence. Lauren asserts in her autobiographical narrative, "Tomorrow I'll try to please him—him and the community and God. So last night, I dreamed a reminder that it's all a lie" (Butler *PS*, ch. 1). Unlike the slave narrative that, as Olney observes, must adhere to the past so that the present audience will accept facts about American enslavement, Butler's work is one of

Afrofuturism, so the destiny of African Americans is key to her message. In effect, Olney's observation is somewhat shortsighted: Douglass, at one point in his narrative, makes reference to his writing in process and how, as he was working on this narrative, he looks down at his feet to seeing the frostbite scars left from his childhood. This brief moment provides Douglass's reader a glimpse into his past and his present, signifying the mental and physical traumas that remain after freedom is obtained.

The past, present, and future are combined in Lauren's journal: in her discussion of her father's Baptist god, Lauren documents that her description has been revised twenty-five to thirty times before the final project is achieved. Her proclamation that God may be redefined, that God is no longer stagnant and is ever-changing, matches the new lives of the American people. In an American slave narrative, the opening statement regarding birth is "a reminder" that enslaved people are born into slavery, that there is no freedom unless they flee North. Olney further delineates the slave narrative structure, noting the presence of the phrase "written by himself" as part of the text's title. According to Olney in reference to Douglass's narrative and the aforementioned title phrase, "it is literally part of the narrative, becoming an important thematic element in the retelling of the life wherein literacy, identity, and a sense of freedom are all acquired simultaneously" (156). Lauren's journal logs her existence for posterity, establishes who she is, and shows the fluidity of her identity and her life. Unlike Lauren's journal, which exists as the narrative's structure, Kendra's entries are imbedded within the story, her voices alternating with that of the male protagonist. Barnes and Due embrace the ensemble structure popular with young adult novelists, but with a price. Butler's novel is cutting edge—Lauren (and Butler) have the courage to expose themselves, flaws and all, to the reader via the journal, offering them the vicarious opportunity to be strong and to survive alongside them. Kendra retreats within her journal, using it as a cocoon from the outside world rather than a space for personal and spiritual growth. With both the slave narrative and the neo-slave narrative, the objective conclusively is to learn about the protagonist's future, one that forefronts the bravery and endurance of the protagonist. Regarding the slave narrative, the outcome for the formerly enslaved person is concrete for the reader once the text begins. The Robledo community offers the illusion of safety, of freedom; for Lauren, there is always the world outside of the walls that offer new possibilities, and Robledo is a place of restriction. Butler's Lauren has few opportunities, but one avails itself promptly with the initial journal entries: Lauren's destiny lies not just outside of her community's walls but in paradisical outer space. Butler's inclusion of an adolescent narrator challenges the precepts of the slave narrative and the neo-slave narrative. The journey to adulthood (the path to freedom) incorporated in the slave narrative is emulated in the young adult neo-slave narrative and in Butler's *PS*. Butler, however, does not cease the journey once freedom has been obtained; she ventures further to offer infinite positive possibilities for African American women. Even though Butler has included an adolescent narrator in *PS*, the subject matter for her work and her formulation of such is mature, thereby, showing the fluid nature of the adolescent reader. There has been criticism regarding young adult literary subject matter, most recently from author Roseanne A. Brown, who, in a tweet, contends that adolescent readers should be exposed to trauma, as it is an issue of which they are aware because it is something that they experience. Whether readers classify Butler's *PS* novel as adult or young adult Afrofuturism, it is a poignant novel that appeals to both age groups due to the sophisticated writing and prevailing substance.

Through the course of the initial novel, Lauren documents her transformation from an individual, an adolescent questioning her societal precepts and her upbringing, to a community leader. Butler channels the adolescent as she creates Lauren, but it must be remembered that Butler's novel is a neo-slave narrative. As with the slave narrative, the structure contains the protagonist recollecting their life, including their early years, as they reflect on previous life-altering events from an adult's standpoint. Lauren stresses that she wishes to please her father, her community, and the Christian God, but she is torn, as these are not her beliefs. When honest with herself and her readers, she comprehends that it is unlikely that she is able to accept that which contradicts her own beliefs, as she disagrees with the formation of her community and their ideology. In truth, Lauren has a sense of foreboding regarding the state of the Robledo community and its stability. She recounts her first dream of flying, which is tied to her second, where she reveals she has learned from her stepmother at seven years old that past Californian society was technologically progressive. In a discussion of late twentieth-century "spacetime travelers," Moylan notes that they "struggle to make sense of their world and to act decisively within it" (*Scraps* 4). A birthday is a moment of normality, as is doing laundry and staring at the stars, which is what Lauren remembers of her early life. Moylan further observes, "At the very least, they act in the name of self-interested effort to be more fully themselves in a difficult place, but more often they strive to be actively part of a found community of people who are also dislocated, and no doubt dispossessed and disempowered" (*Scraps* 4). The chapter concludes with Butler foreshadowing Lauren's desire for the Earthseed followers that their future rests not on Earth, but in space.

Lauren is dissatisfied with the Robledo community and their beliefs, foreshadowing her eventual departure from such. It has been well documented by theorists analyzing young adult literature that this genre concentrates on the protagonist's refutation of the adult societal construction; it must be pointed out that these theorists are working with texts about the Caucasian adolescent experience. While Butler has accomplished the aforementioned journey for Lauren, she has ensured that Lauren's intersectionality has been presented. In keeping with the Afrofuturist vision and the slave narrative plot structure, (a) African Americans must be shown as part of the future, and (b) the central figure must become a leader of the movement, a champion for those continuing to be oppressed. Even though this example refers to a Caucasian protagonist, a parallel may be witnessed between Lauren and Katniss. In the initial two novels in the Hunger Games series, Katniss rebels against the Capitol's hierarchy, while the third deals with Katniss morphing from individual to leader of the rebellion. Both Lauren and Katniss become more than lone persons immersed in their respective societies; they become symbols for entire movements.

Lauren's foray into her past continues with a diary entry about her baptism in her father's religion, something that she disagrees with, but completes the ritual even though it makes her feel hypocritical. Surrounded by a dangerous dystopic space, Lauren spends her first few diary entries behaving as a normal adolescent, warring within herself as to whose ideology should be asserted, hers or her father's. Lauren gets baptized into the Baptist faith to appease her father, the Baptist minister, and to refrain from causing any conflict within her community as others also were to undergo the same ritual. Reality intercedes once the group exits the Robledo community and ventures past the wall into dystopic Los Angeles. Lauren's entry is filled with observations about women and children who are poverty-stricken and worse—raped and drug addled. While Lauren's brother, Keith, finds going outside of Robledo's walls exciting, in traditional slave narrative fashion, the male experience differs from that of the female as it is she who must fear more from outside forces, namely the violation of her body through rape. It is on this day that the reader learns about Lauren's condition, one that Barnes and Due attempt to replicate in their series among other attributes of Butler's character and the novel's plot points.

The day after her birthday, Lauren is on her way to get baptized, an event symbolic of a new stage of life. As she cycles by, she sees homeless persons and wishes she could do something to help. Lauren writes, "I can take a lot of pain without falling apart. I've had to learn to do that. But it was hard, today, to keep peddling and keep up with the others when just about everyone I saw made me feel worse and worse" (Butler *PS*, ch. 2). This is the initial indication that Lauren differs from her adolescent community for reasons other than the standard for people her age. Readers immediately identify that Lauren disagrees with her father's beliefs; discord within the familial unit is normal for a person of Lauren's age as she identifies her own belief system. As she progresses throughout the novel, Lauren reveals that she is unique, a difference that enables her to successfully establish the Acorn survivalist community. Science fiction writers commonly offer parallels in their writing to that of real-world society; as she goes with her adolescent community to be baptized, Lauren reveals that she has hyperempathy syndrome. Lauren's medical condition resulted from a drug that her mother took when she was pregnant and, as a result, Lauren is a person of disability. Since Butler wrote her novel in the late 1990s and had noted that she created Duryea-Gode disease in "The Evening and the Morning and the Night" based on an authentic disease, it is feasible that the Thalidomide crisis of the 1960s aided in her creation of Lauren. By doing so, Butler includes a real fear that women have, that the prescription drug, Paracetco, that her birth mother takes while pregnant has caused her hyperempathy. In her writings, Butler creates numerous people of disability, thereby offering characters that stand out as individuals who become successful because of, not despite, their differences. It is Lauren's syndrome that aids in her creation of the Earthseed doctrine and subsequent Acorn community, that aids in her becoming a leader and a survivor. Butler's Lauren offers a vision of positivity for adolescent and adult readers alike, while Barnes and Due's novel contains stereotyping regarding gender and ethnicity that gives the audience a poor look at twenty-first-century youth.

KENDRA, STEREOTYPES, AND ZOMBIES

It is commonly understood that William Shakespeare based many of his plays on source texts, stories written by Greek and Roman writers such as Plautus and Terrance. In the twenty-first century, writers still use source materials (intertextuality) and when they do so—for example, *Pride and Prejudice and Zombies*—they tend to acknowledge within their adaptations that they have based their novels on someone else's material. It is glaringly obvious that Barnes and Due have utilized Butler's Parable series, in particular *PS*, as source material for their own series. There are far too many commonalities between the two texts for this to be an analytical error, and no acknowledgment that Butler's work has guided the duo in the creation of this series has been located.

FAMILY AND VACCINES IN THE NEO-SLAVE NARRATIVE

As is consistent with the slave narrative, both Barnes and Due's *DW* and Butler's *PS* begin with an introduction to the protagonist's family, or lack thereof. So that the formerly enslaved person's voice is deemed credible by the predominantly White readership, the slave narrative opens with an introduction to the formerly enslaved person's background. While it was commonplace in the nineteenth century for White individuals to present a letter of introduction, thereby garnering acceptable from their peers, this societal construction does not apply for the formerly enslaved. Rather, the start of the narrative included this familial information, including the statement regarding birth, so that the White audience would see that the timeline of events is valid and, critically, that the readers may make emotional contact with the writer. The enslaved or formerly enslaved were reliant on the empowered abolitionists, so commonalities in experience—the enslaved are humans not property and they have families also—may stir the empathy of the abolitionists.

Starting with Kendra, *DW* opens with her listening to news reports regarding outbreaks of violent behavior in various locales, including a boarding school in New Jersey. On their way to the hospital Kendra's mother, Cassandra Brookings, is exasperated by Kendra's constant objections to the flu vaccine while her father, Devon, tries to soothe her fears. Immediately, if examining *DW* in accordance with Sargent's guidelines, it is apparent that Barnes and Due's novel is dystopic. Like Lauren, Kendra is introduced surrounded by a loving family. Kendra's life coach/family therapist parents, Cassandra and Devon, are described as physically attractive, doting parents who only want the best for their daughter. The narrator portrays Kendra as feeling suffocated by her parents; Barnes and Due have created a seemingly ideal family for Kendra. The characters are, unfortunately, unrealistic in their saccharine portrayal. Lauren, however, is part of a blended family: stepmother Corey, brother Keith, and her father. Her family is flawed as are the characters, which makes them more relatable for the reader. Connecting the novels to the slave narrative and African American literature in general, the family is a significant entity. As I showed in my article "Liberation through Acceptance of Nature and Technology in Octavia E. Butler's 'Parable of the Sower,'" Lauren is accepting of others, meeting and helping people on her way to what becomes the Earthseed community. While the African American woman is often typecast as the caregiver figure (see chapter 1), Butler refutes the stereotype, making Lauren both a caring individual and one that is a leader for her newly formed community. She further ensures that Lauren is knowledgeable about her family and her past, but only to a certain point. She is aware that her biological mother took a drug during her pregnancy that resulted in Lauren's syndrome, but is accepting of her actions and the results. Lauren is a person of disability who is presented realistically; she is not superhuman or incapable of action, rather she comprehends who she is, and this identity includes limitations brought on by her syndrome.

In *DW*, the writers included the nuclear family, a societal construct connected to the White middle class. By refuting the stereotype of the African American fractured family, Barnes and Due include a favorable aspect in their novel, one that works to make the "traditional," functional African American two parent and child(ren) visible. This is not to say that there is anything wrong with a blended family for African American people or anyone from another racial background; instead, due to the stereotype of the African American absentee father and the "broken" family, Barnes and Due's storyline works to counter these hurtful images. Applying intersectionality to her analysis, Sherell A. McArthur discusses the change needed in education for Black girls: "Centering Black girls' lived experience through critical media literacy can teach critical thinking and interrogation and enables Black girls to negotiate visibility by counternarrating racist, sexist, and classist media narratives with authentic stories of Black girlhood" (362). How Barnes and Due create their characters belies the optimism felt in connection to Kendra's family construction. The narrator describes Kendra's mother—"Cassandra Brookings had the cheekbones and carriage that said 'runway' even if she'd opted for owlish glasses and a family therapist's credentials" (*DW* 4)—contradicting the realism of the family's construction. The nuclear African American family is shown by Barnes and Due as a façade rather than authentic, their presentation of the family sending a negative message to the adolescent reader, Black or another racial identity, instead of normalizing the image. As McArthur and Crenshaw in her article for *MS.* magazine show, it is Black girls that necessitate the need for change because it is they who are consistently typecast and omitted from public visibility. In many cases, some of which have been documented in this book, Black young women have been marginalized and if they are portrayed in a favorable light, their visibility is brief. Kendra's family is unbelievable not because of the portrayal of the united family but because of the falsity of the character construction. Crenshaw affirms the stereotypes that Black girls face, documenting how Black girls in the United States have been treated with suspicion and violence in educational spaces. In "Black Girls Matter," Crenshaw divulges the numerous cases in the United States of Black adolescent girls who have been subjected to violence, victimized because of their racial and gender identity. Crenshaw continues, explaining that Black males receive assistance due to their marginalized state, but because of "Black male exceptionalism," Black girls are neglected, not recognized as needing help. Melissa V. Harris-Perry asserts, "They [Black women's experiences] are political because black women in America have always had to wrestle with derogatory assumptions about their character and identity" (5). Black women are typed as strong Black women, thereby able to care for themselves and others; because of the construct, they many times are ignored and, in fact, further marginalized. The characters' appearance is key to their understanding of their respective identities and the message that Barnes and Due are offering their adolescent readership. In order to break a stereotype, reality not idealization should be emphasized, especially when writing to a twenty-first-century adolescent readership. Regarding African American women, more than one stereotype must be shattered, for example, the Mammy, the Jezebel, the angry Black woman, and the Sapphire. As academics we must be cognizant of the constructs about Black women that exist and must also work to identify them, so that they can no longer be perpetuated. As Harris-Perry shows in her examination of the *Sex and the City* film and Jennifer Hudson's character (78–79), even in the twenty-first century Black women are faced with typecasting. Further, referencing the characters of Cassandra and Devon, the mother character is described as physically beautiful "even if she'd opted for owlish glasses and a family therapist's credentials" (4) while her father is described as a former athlete who has gained some weight. Cassandra is not permitted to be physically attractive as well as smart and successful, and "Devon Brookings was a big man in his mid-forties, a college athlete who now enjoyed couches more than wind sprints" (*DW* 4), thereby channeling the Sambo stereotype.

The physicality of the character is present in the novel, an attribute that African American people have been attempting to reclaim. The idealized family is shown at surface level only, sending a detrimental message to readers about the African American family, one that has been consistently perpetuated. This disregard of positive African American images continues in the family's conversation about the vaccination and Kendra's fears of getting one.

While Lauren is shown to the reader after a catastrophic event has occurred—the economic downfall of the United States—Kendra's threat revolves around her mistrust of the flu vaccination, thereby seeming to capitalize on the anti-vaxxer ideology. During the COVID-19 pandemic and the subsequent vaccinations of the American people, African American people's fears of vaccinations came to light once more. Vice president Kamala Harris had her coronavirus vaccination visually recorded, thereby attempting to alleviate African Americans' concerns about having the vaccination. Due to the Tuskegee Study of Untreated Syphilis in the Negro Male, one which continued for forty years, many African American men suffered needlessly as they were unknowingly experimented on. Henrietta Lacks had her cancer cells removed at Johns Hopkins Hospital, unknowingly having them used for study. African Americans have concerns about medical treatments because of medical abuses perpetuated against them. Kendra's parents refuse to take her fears about the vaccination seriously; on the surface it appears that this moment in the novel is about parents ignoring their adolescent's irrational fears. Later, as Kendra recounts her family escaping the hospital's zombies, Kendra gives her written gratitude to God, claiming that he made it possible for her to avoid the vaccination. While the starting point of each novel slightly differs, Lauren is in California and Kendra in Washington, both are still set on the West Coast and contain an element of fear about Western medicine. Lauren lives in constant fear that the users of the drug Pyro will invade their compound and shows the blind trust that women had in their physicians in the twentieth century. Kendra asserts an authentic fear about medical treatments as an African American person, but she is disregarded as an adolescent by her parents. Even though Butler gives Lauren a made-up condition, the threat a birth mother faces regarding the ingestion of drugs, while deemed to be safe, is real and Butler is acting responsibly toward her adolescent readers. Barnes and Due write about people that get the flu vaccine which, when combined with a special diet, turns them into zombies. Is it responsible for authors writing for a YA audience to confirm Kendra's fears about getting a flu vaccine? Or is it more troubling that the fears an African American person has about unknown medical treatments are not discussed and are disregarded as a child's worry? The concern felt about the Black body's violation is a valid one. As there are so few YA science fiction authors writing about female protagonists of African descent, do writers have more of an obligation to their readers to provide socially responsible material? Not to mention, should a female lead not be courageous rather than complacent?

KENDRA AND LAUREN'S SYNDROMES

Kendra mentally and physically shuts down each time there is a traumatic event, her hyperempathy making it more difficult for her to function, as she is in constant pain. Unlike Lauren, who quickly learns to protect herself from harm, Kendra ceases to interact with society, preferring to have others care for her. Whereas Lauren explains her hyperempathy to her readers, showing how it impacts her experiences, the linkage between Kendra's syndrome and actions is rarely explained. When Kendra goes for her flu shot, her father is attacked by a zombie in the Portland General hospital and her parents must physically drag Kendra out to the car. At eighteen years of age, Lauren witnesses the destruction of her Robledo community; she escapes, ensuring that her survival pack is with her when she goes, only to return the next day in order to search for her family. Once it is discovered that her family is dead, she joins with a few survivors and ventures to Northern California, where she will eventually establish Acorn. Kendra's parents attempt to get her out of the door of the hospital and to safety while she fights them so that she may go the other way. The narrator reveals that "Kendra wasn't thinking—her brain had shut down, body reduced to primeval drives": she does not try to save herself or aid in her family's escape (Barnes and Due *DW*, ch. 2). Understandably, adolescent Kendra would be distressed and traumatized by the zombie attack, particularly as it directly affects her family. The contention is not being made here that young adult novelists should provide their primarily adolescent readers with an idealized character; instead, they should include one that is flawed—a realistic character that is able to offer to readers understanding about age-specific trials.

Connecting these plot segments to the slave narrative, historian Dea H. Boster has extensively examines the Black body and disability during American enslavement. Boster informs her reader that many formerly enslaved persons were physically scarred by their enslavers and by their environment. The enslaved's exploitation continues as the abolitionists placed their physical bodies on display, used as an example of the South's atrocities. As Boster tells, "In the 1840s and 1850s, many antislavery audiences were fascinated with the experiences of disabled slave bodies, and detailed accounts of slaves who sustained terrible, debilitating injuries during their bondage were abundant in abolitionist speeches and publications" (1). The physicality of the Black body is visible to the audience, but the emotions of the formerly enslaved are hidden. The body is used to demonstrate to antislavery activists for whom they should be speaking: Boster likens their bodies utilized in this way to the method in which the enslaved are sold at slave auctions (1). Expanding on these tableaus, Boster informs the reader that "on many occasions, the ex-slaves remained largely silent, appearing before the audience only to agree with the main presenters about the facts of their cases or to present their injuries" (1). The formerly enslaved are objectified, the further desecration of the Black body perpetuated by their lack of speech. Even though it was unseemly for White bodies to show skin in the nineteenth century, Black bodies of both sexes revealed the places that they were assaulted, removing clothing in order to do so (Boster 1). Enslaved, lacking control over their own bodies and voices, the violations continue even in freedom. Ultimately, formerly enslaved persons of disability are silenced, the physical presence of the abolitionists acting as the authenticating documents from the slave narrative. The formerly enslaved are actors in their own narratives; yet, Boster's portrayal of people with disabilities as well as Kimberly Snyder Manganelli's depiction of Douglass and other formerly enslaved persons' trips to London (69) reveals that they were subjected to the gaze of White European persons.

Lauren's disability is not something of which she is ashamed, but it is kept secret, as it makes her different from others in her community. Differing from the accepted norm in Lauren's dystopic space makes her a target of those inside and outside of Robledo's walls. For Lauren, her hyperempathy is an invisible disability, one that may only be visually witnessed when she gets too close to another person emotionally. For example, her brother Keith cuts himself while she watches, and she bleeds. Her father is domineering, refusing to accept Lauren's disability and hiding it, as if ashamed. As an adolescent, Lauren is mature for her age, transcending the racism and discrimination that exists in her community. Lauren has been conditioned to believe that her disability is not real, that it is an illusion that she needs to overcome; she elaborates, "Anyway, my neurotransmitters are scrambled and they're going to stay scrambled. But I can do okay as long as other people don't know about me" (Butler 12). Lauren is placed on display for her community, not because her disability as the grotesque but because her father wants her to be an example for others in their community as someone who has overcome adversity. Lauren's father asserts the normal/abnormal binary often found in Butler's prose. Over time, Lauren accepts who she is, but not until she leaves Robledo is she comfortable with her identity. Butler portrays Lauren's disability as a strength, one that aids in her creation of a sustainable and equitable community. The reader must be cautioned as Butler is not re-creating the Mammy stereotype here (self-sacrificing for others), nor is she writing a character who "overcomes" their disability—another stereotype. Rather, Lauren is depicted as representational, as a leader of a community that refuses conformity.

ZOMBIES, CHARACTERIZATION, AND NARRATION

The utilization of the zombie figure in the novels adds an intriguing yet ineffective alteration to the source text's victims of Pyro. Kawin extensively documents the appearance of the zombie in the horror genre, citing that zombies are divided into two groupings with their own respective traits (118). Kawin reveals that regarding media representation, the initial zombie incarnation is the Haitian zombie. Zora Neale Hurston, eminent novelist and anthropologist, went to Haiti on a Guggenheim fellowship, working on "a study of magic practices among Negroes of the West Indies" (King *African Americans*, 276). Not only are Hurston's fictional writings some of the most impactful contributions to the Harlem Renaissance and the American canon overall, but also her *Tell My Horse* (1938), an account of her trip to Haiti and her explorations about voodoo, is an insightful analysis of a society that includes the zombie—the authentic zombie. Kawin labels Haitian zombies "mindless slaves" (118). Hurston shows that they exist as part of a religious practice, that they are present in twentieth-century society and are remnants of actual people rather than monsters. After delving into Wade Thomas's *The Serpent and the Rainbow* (1985), Kawin debunks the Hollywood construct of the Haitian zombie: "The movies have shown little interest in anthropologically rigorous approaches to Haitian culture or religion. They have taken the concept of the zombie, the mindless walking dead, and run with it" (118). The author's investigation into the two types of zombies (the Haitian adaptation and George A. Romero's zombies), especially those capitalized on in film as those zombies are the ones with which people are most enamored, is relevant to the *DW* novel as it is implied that both characterizations have been included. Kawin documents, as others have done, that the second and later incarnation of the zombie is created by Romero: "Romero's [horror films] set good against evil (often in a human battle) and us against a version of ourselves (the zombies)" (120). The mirroring technique that Kawin acknowledges—that humanity's worst traits are shown in the zombies—has been emulated by Barnes and Due. The freaks, as Kendra's group have named the zombies, are, as traditionally constructed, symbolic of consumption. While on the group's journey to the supposedly utopic space in California—a trope that Ireland also utilizes in her Dread Nation series—the voices of others in their community are occasionally inserted, thereby revealing a collective point of view regarding the state of society. By adding the others in the group as storytellers, the narrative structure works to make *DW* more inclusive and personal as the adolescents are then permitted to comment on events unfolding. The intent is to create a cohesive community, to include other characters' voices, but the structure disappoints. Later in the novel, when the group reaches California and the third-person narrator directs the reader to Terry's emotional experiences, it is temporary. The omniscient narrator enables readers to learn about the entire group, but it does not unify them: "Kendra realized that she and Ursalina might be the only two people on the bus who had seen someone they loved bitten by freaks. They hadn't been squirreled away at a camp in the woods" (*DW*, 242–43). Rather than retaining the first-person only narrative style of Butler's *PS* or the slave narrative, Barnes and Due apply the alternating narrator structure that works to show dissention within the group.

Kendra's story is interrupted by the third-person narrator, enabling readers to witness the male protagonist's experiences. Terry is portrayed as a cross between a juvenile delinquent and a misunderstood adolescent. After many criminal acts, Terry is shown choosing to work at a youth camp rather than being incarcerated. With the stereotypes that abound about African American males, it is disturbing that Barnes and Due would choose to make their African American male protagonist a young offender. Throughout the novel, when Terry's point of view is offered, he is portrayed as having a tough exterior, yet he cares about others. Stereotypes abound in *DW*, as he is portrayed as the bad boy type that may be reformed by an overemotional good girl. Both protagonists discover each other when their society suffers an apocalyptic catastrophe: people are turned into zombies due to the combination of the flu shot and a weight loss remedy.

Once the narrative structure shifts back to Kendra after Terry is introduced, Lauren is once again emulated as Kendra has begun to write her story down in a diary. For Lauren, her journals are the start of the Earthseed religion and a method of saving humanity from extinction. Lauren is an authentic activist, as she comprehends at an early age that societal disruption that is occurring concerns not only her but everyone. Her perspective is all-encompassing, as she looks outward rather than inward, unlike Kendra, who wishes to record events. Kendra's entry in chapter 4 reveals to the reader that she learned the art of journaling from a teacher and that this method of self-exploration is supposed to aid in her awareness of her trauma. The first-person narrator should solicit empathy from the audience, as Kendra is an adolescent experiencing earthshattering events, like the transformation of people into zombies. Her behavior, however, is disdainful as she compares the zombie invasion to 9/11, a mass casualty terrorist attack that continuously affects Americans. Instead of portraying their adolescent in a realistic and relatable manner, the authors have Kendra's state, "I had to stop and take a nap. They're saying not to let bit people go to sleep, but I wasn't bit. Hope it's all right if I just curl up and let the world go away for a while," which is uninspiring (Barnes and Due, *DW* 21). Both Kendra and her father, who has been bitten by a zombie, desire to sink into nothingness; while Dev is dying, Kendra is incapacitated by her fear of the unknown. Forcing a character to ignore their grief is not the issue here, but as the character is repeatedly in great peril, it is concerning that Kendra enacts behavior that could cause her death. Kendra's behavior is similar to what Kawin asserts about Romero's zombies (120): the zombies show Kendra as a shadow of her former self. She refuses to heal in the novel, continuing to resent her parents even after their deaths; she reveals that her parents should have trusted her about the flu vaccination. Kendra continues to document her devastation after the death of her parents, and her diary entries are a way for her to cope with the implosion of her world. It is appreciated that Barnes and Due give readers a character that has the ability to self-soothe in times of crisis through the use of her writing; however, her constant uncertainty and fragility combined make her an unlikable stereotype of a female character. When the group ventures deep into California and meets Sharon Lampher, the visually impaired seer, it becomes apparent that Barnes and Due have chosen to make Kendra psychic. Lauren creates a community, aiding the others in a journey of self-acceptance, one that transcends humanity's Earthen space. Kendra, however, becomes a magical being, one that behaves foolishly until the close of the second novel. The adult, Ursula, reprimands Kendra for kissing Terry, who has been infected with the zombie virus. *Domino Falls* concludes with Kendra's regrets as she flies away with the remainder of her friends.

CONCLUSION

When Kendra is found by Terry, she has just resigned herself to her fate. After she thinks to herself, "Might as well just stay here, curled up in the dark. Wait to die" (*DW* 124), Kendra goes into the fetal position. Katharine Capshaw Smith analyzes Harlem Renaissance children's literature, noting, "Children's literature in the 1910s, 1920s, and 1930s drew its energy from the multiple currents of uplift ideology, its birth a result . . . of the tensions between Du Bois's faith in an edifying home life, insistence on liberal arts education, desire for white recognition, and resistance to the protectionist ideology espoused by the black elite" (xvi).[4] I am not recommending a return to this structure for contemporary African American YA literature; instead, I am pointing out the challenges associated with creating literature that disparages African American female adolescents. Once she joins her group rather than becoming a leader like Lauren, Kendra is the "heart" of the group of adolescents—it is disconcerting that Barnes and Due have created an emotional female adolescent who spends her time crying. In one instance, Kendra shows that she is jealous of her new friend, Sonia, for entering a relationship with another male character, Piranha; Kendra wishes for the protection, for the safety of a male but wonders about having to prostitute herself for that protection. When the bus reaches California, Kendra repeatedly places her hand on Terry's thigh, enjoying her nearness to him. Terry's response to her actions, to her statement that she is not a "kid" and to her forwardness, is to state, "You're going to get me arrested" (*DW* 246). When they meet the Californian community members at the checkpoint, Terry reveals himself to be the leader, taking charge and speaking for the group. Kendra remains voiceless, only once professing knowledge when she tells the men that they are looking for Devil's Wake island. Terry quickly corrects Kendra about their intended destination, Domino Falls, a supposed utopia. In addition, Kendra affirms her passivity and her position as a stereotype of an adolescent girl when Terry inquires into the state of Reverend Meeks's community; she is pleased that they have had similar observations, but Kendra does not verbalize her ideas. Kendra shows her strength when she asks Reverend Meeks to pray for her group, revealing that—like Lauren—Kendra represents hope.

Devil's Wake contains a collection of stereotypes, and the female and male characters are riddled with negative gender constructs. Butler's novel, however, embodies the spirit of Afrofuturism as set out by Dery, who first coined the term, and incorporates elements of Kilgore's elaboration. Readers witness a decisive and confident African American female protagonist who leads the remainder of humanity to a positive future. Lauren rejects the stereotypes of female slaves, including the constructed idealization of the female slave. Lauren is not embodied as the caregiver, but rather she exists as the voice of future generations—she is a leader. Kendra embodies the adolescent attempting to transition from such to a functioning adult. Unfortunately, Barnes and Due's construction falls flat, as Kendra's character is ineffective and far from being a leader and role model.

Chapter 4

THE BIRACIAL FEMALE PROTAGONIST, TRAUMA, AND MEMORY IN A. J. HARTLEY'S *STEEPLEJACK*

INTRODUCTION: THE WHITE WRITER AND THE BIRACIAL CHARACTER

In much of the science fiction genre, including twenty-first-century young adult contributions, a character's racial identification tends to be casually observed to the reader, or it may be alluded to by the writer rather than explicitly shown. In reference to twentieth-century science fiction, Leonard observes that characters' default race tends to be Caucasian; here, Leonard refers to science fiction narratives directed to an adult audience, but the same may be said of young adult. Couzelis examines the young adult dystopian novel, agreeing with Leonard; she also calls attention to the fact that not only are "racial tensions . . . often not [explicitly] addressed in futuristic novels" but also "ideologies about race are present in the narratives" (131). In the early twenty-first century, a point of contention among YA readers was Katniss's ethnicity in the series the Hunger Games and the subsequent portrayal of the character by Jennifer Lawrence, a Caucasian actor, in the cinematic version. Another dispute arose in 2016 when a Black actor was cast to play Hermione in J. K. Rowling's *Harry Potter and the Cursed Child*.[1] While there was some support for Noma Dumezweni being cast in this role, including from Rowling herself, others came out on social media and expressed their racist outrage that Hermione was not to be played by a White actor. Rowling makes it clear in her interview with *The Guardian* (June 2016) that "there is no reason why Hermione should be white" and, notably, her ethnicity does not appear to be given at all in the series of texts

(Ratcliffe). In point of fact, A. J. Hartley solicited Dumezweni to be the reader for his audiobook version of the novel being examined here, a job she took. In an article in *The Atlantic*, award-winning YA author Coe Booth discusses her love for Judy Blume's books and the stereotypical appearance of African American characters in 1960s' young adult literature. When Booth delves into an examination of twenty-first-century YA characters, she observes that in some cases they are "white by default.... You see books where the character is black, and they have these long descriptions about skin color and so on. That's so irritating; you never do that if they're white" (Doll). Booth continues to cite problems in YA with regards to ethnicity, stating that when authors do include characters of color they face pressures that other writers do not. Often African American writers have reported that they feel forced to write only about African American culture and incidents of racism. Couzelis agrees, noting, "Often when novels for general audiences address race effectively, they are almost always read as solely 'about race' and become marginalized, thereby avoiding critical engagement by mainstream audiences" (132).

However, in the young adult speculative fiction novel *Steeplejack* (2016) from British writer Hartley, the author places great emphasis on race and race relations in his society of Bar-Selehm. Before delving into an examination of the initial novel in his Steeplejack trilogy, we as readers must be cognizant of Hartley's racial and gender identification, both of which unduly impact any writer's creative output.[2] In his blog post "Writing POC While White," Hartley lays out why he has chosen to create a biracial protagonist for the lead in his Steeplejack series. Offering to writers advice about what not to do, namely embracing racist characterizations and "assum[ing] that race/ethnicity is irrelevant, so characters can be written as white and then (like the awful colorizing of old movies) given a superficial tint"—Hartley explains that race is part of one's identity. Further documenting the anti-Asian attitude that has long existed in the United States, which culminated with a great deal of anti-Asian violence in connection to COVID-19 in 2020–2021, Hartley states that his wife, who identifies as Asian, and biracial child have both experienced discriminatory behavior. In reference to his writing, Hartley states, "I don't claim to be an expert, but I am committed to giving diverse characters my very best shot, while simultaneously supporting marginalized writers in the telling of their own stories" ("Writing POC"). In the refrain that has been echoing across social media—"We can do better"—Hartley has attempted to do just that with *Steeplejack*.

In his neo-Victorian novel *Steeplejack* (the first novel in his Tor published trilogy) and its short story prequel "Chains," Hartley centers his texts on the seventeen-year-old Lani female steeplejack Anglet (Ang) Sutonga. Ang is a rarity in her society as she is a Lani female steeplejack; she is subject to societal discrimination with regards to her gender, race, class, and job. Hartley has also written an article for Tor.com, citing his upbringing in Lancashire as an important influence on his creation of the Ang character, namely Hartley's making Ang a steeplejack. Hartley defines a "steepleclimber," later to be called a steeplejack or chimney sweep, as "the guys who used systems of ladders and ropes to scale those otherwise inaccessible structures to fix up what the regular masons wouldn't go near" ("A Head for Heights"). Readers should take notice of Hartley's usage of the word "guys" as he describes who it is that takes this position, which started in the eighteenth century and concluded in the late twentieth. Importantly, Hartley alters the traditional gender identity of the steeplejack, making Ang female, another method of calling attention to societal marginalization.

Regarding location, while Hartley has stated that his novel has been inspired by South Africa and Swaziland, there is some latitude to examine the novel's racial politics through an Americanist and British lens, especially since Hartley's English upbringing impacted the novel's setting. In describing his urban creation of Bar-Selehm, Hartley is ambiguous, citing a melding of cultures and spaces: "The city looks a bit like South Africa but looks more like Victorian London than South Africa ever did, and its political system looks more like apartheid than like the early years of colonialism" ("Writing POC"). Ang's society is divided by race: Lani (described by Ang as having a brown complexion), White people, and Mahweni people (Black persons); and gender identity: male and female. Hartley furthers divides his society by categorizing the Mahweni into Assimilated and Unassimilated people. While the American slave narrative primarily delineates the experiences of enslaved people born into enslavement, the British slave narrative concentrates on enslaved people who have most likely been taken from their homes and forced into enslavement.

Due to Ang's traumatic experiences and the societal construction stemming from second-generational memories of the past, she has difficulty changing her oppressed state. In order for Ang to recognize her societal position as object, as an enslaved person, and change it, she must recognize the racist and sexist societal structure in place and then work toward rejecting this structure. Further, Ang must acknowledge and utilize her trauma as a tool to remove her from her oppressed state. *Steeplejack* has been examined as an American slave narrative, focusing on the protagonist's efforts to ensure the continuance of the community, which is a primary facet of the female slave narrative.

SECOND-GENERATIONAL MEMORY AND ITS ILL EFFECTS ON SOCIETAL CONSTRUCTION

Anastasia Ulanowicz,[3] in her monograph *Second-Generation Memory and Contemporary Children's Literature: Ghost Images*, posits that an adjustment should be made to the theory of inherited memories. Ulanowicz, who has thoroughly explored the conceptualization of inherited memory, writes, "Identified in other critical contexts as 'postmemory' (Marianne Hirsh), 'prosthetic memory' (Alison Landsberg), 'belated witness' (Michael Levine), and 'second-generation witness' (Alan Berger), this form of inherited or vicarious memory has been of considerable interest to scholars who theorize an order of memory that is not predicated upon direct experience" (6). While the theorists with which Ulanowicz works utilize the memory primarily in connection to the Holocaust, Ulanowicz expands her genre analysis, incorporating 9/11. Ulanowicz focuses her examination on children's literature outputs, specifically those that directly deal with the tragedy associated with the aforementioned traumatic events. Further, Ulanowicz provides the reader with the rationale behind her alteration to the memory concepts and the need for a new term to describe inherited memory. As Ulanowicz provides, the concept of postmemory is problematic, as the prefix "post" implies that which has occurred instead of continuously having an impact on the holder of the memories (8). Ulanowicz elaborates: "Memory is a function of the imagination. Formulated in the aftermath of an unrepeatable past, memory can only reconstruct, or re-imagine, what can never be fully present again" (8). When analyzing the neo-slave narrative construction, there should be recognition paid to the application of memory to this genre's construction.

In Morison's *Beloved*, one of the author's most famous characters, Sethe, attempts to describe in order to teach her daughter, Denver, about using language to come to terms with the past:

> I was talking about time. It's so hard for me to believe in it. Some things go. Pass on. Some things just stay. I used to think it was my rememory. You know. Some things you forget. Other things you never do. But it's not. Places, places are still there. If a house burns down, it's gone, but the place—the picture of it—stays, and not just in my rememory, but out there, in the world. What I remember is a picture floating around out there outside my head. I mean, even if I don't think it, even if I die, the picture of what I did, or knew, or saw is still out there. Right in the place where it happened. (Morrison *Beloved*, 35)

Sethe tells her daughter that it is not praying that can help her accept and eventually release the turmoil of emotions and memories that continue to repeat for her. The character of Sethe voices the feelings of African American people that are shown in many literary and media constructions, that the aftereffects of American enslavement are inescapable. It is only once Sethe voices her reality to others in her community and that same community comes to her aid that she is able to accept the ghosts of enslavement, symbolically acknowledging that the horrors of enslavement are a part of her identity and her history.

Rushdy, referring to Morrison's concept of rememory, defines this conceptualization as "a way to understand how we can share in the prior experiences of others" (6). He hypothesizes that rememory is an experience that may be had equally, no matter the experiencer's time, and that the past affects the present (7). Rushdy delineates Morrison's rememory, a concept that originates in a slave narrative integral to the genre and the extent of trauma that the people connected to American enslavement face each day. The repetition that Ulanowicz (8) asserts reverberates throughout the reconstruction and reenvisioning that happens with the young adult neo-slave narrative. Ulanowicz poses that, in order to be affected by the content, the reader need not be from the time of the act, but there must be a generational connection. In defining "generation," Ulanowicz states, "The term 'generation,' in other words, implies a certain *relationality*, insofar as it demarcates a certain demographic with respect to groups that precede and follow it" (9). Ultimately, when reading a neo-slave narrative destined for an adolescent audience, the reader must be aware that the audience may contain descendants of enslaved people and may identify as Black, biracial, or multiracial. Since these texts are for an adolescent audience, there is also the possibility of a diverse and inclusive audience, that the readers may not identify as Black, and the genre works to teach readers via second-generational memory, albeit indirectly (the neo-slave narrative is a written record of second-generation memory), regarding the experiences of enslaved African American people. When dealing with literary outputs directed to an adolescent audience, in general, some writers endeavor to write to a multiracial and multiethnic audience, aiding in creating understanding of racial experiences and empathy among peers. While a reader who is not Black will not have the same experiences with these readings, interacting with neo-slave narratives—creations of second-generational memory—may work toward awareness regarding American enslavement. As a university-level educator, I work to ensure my courses are diverse and inclusive, so as to enable students to empathize with others' experiences, including those obtained not through lived experiences but through second-generational memory.[4]

In examining children's literature, Ulanowicz sees its readers as visionaries, as open to suggestion and to experiencing new events, ultimately learning from others (7). Ulanowicz reports that "second-generation memory involves an individual's conscious recognition of the ways in which her present circumstances have been mediated and shaped by past events that she herself did not directly experience" (4). Referencing Morrison's *Beloved*, Emily Miller Budick refers to Beloved as the past, offering "This past is not simply the private, personal history of Sethe, Denver, and Paul D. insofar as Beloved figures slavery itself, she re-members the history of an entire people" (118). Both Ulanowicz and Budick capture the long-reaching effects of a monumental and life-changing atrocity as is American enslavement of people of African descent. The difference between Ulanowicz and Budick, however, is that the former, while referencing second-generation memory in connection to specific events, engages specifically with its reproduction in children's literature. Instead of protecting children from potentially trauma-inducing events, Ulanowicz reveals that "Whereas once educators and children's authors warned parents against exposing their children to any material that might permanently traumatize them, contemporary children's books—and the educational, psychological, and marketing apparatuses that attend and support them—now practically insist that young people be subjected to disturbing stories of the past" (2). Due to the fantastical yet realistic nature of science fiction and speculative fiction, these genres tend to work well for the presentation of the neo-slave narrative directed toward an adolescent audience. As K. V. Bailey and Andy Sawyer show, there has been a pattern of adolescent works with fantastical elements: "While in the second half of the twentieth-century British writers of hard science fiction for the young adult are fairly thin on the ground, those whose writings reflect a background in fantasy ... are plentiful" (59).[5] Writers combine the slave narrative and the speculative genres in order to reach a contemporary audience, and the speculative genres give writers latitude to approach an incredibly traumatizing event for a new readership—adolescents. Speculative fiction enables Dana to travel through time in order to learn about her family, and for Sethe's baby to haunt her, so that she may have closure. Its wonderous nature permits two African American young women (Jane and Katherine in *Deathless Divide*) to conquer an evil worse than zombies, the White male scientist who abuses Black bodies; to Lauren's creation of a life-saving community; and to Ang's rewriting of history by becoming a biracial female chimney sweep.

Fantastic elements of the neo-slave narrative allow for the reenvisioning of oppressive societal guidelines, thereby permitting Ang's heroic efforts to alter the societal guidelines for women and for people of color in place. Hartley creates Ang, the neo-Victorian chimney sweep, as a descendant of immigrants who are taken to Bar-Selehm as indentured servants. She explains, "The Lani aren't indigenous to the region. We were brought here almost three hundred years ago from lands to the east by the whites from the north" (Hartley *Steeplejack*, 17), but Ang's recollections fluctuate in their decisiveness. As the novel unfolds, Ang delineates Bar-Selehm's societal construction, informing the reader that the majority of steeplejacks are Lani males, while the remainder are made up of poverty-stricken White people and Mahweni outcasts. Further, the Lani men are the leaders of the gangs, a characterization parallel to enslaved people forced by enslavers to inflict violence on other enslaved people. Ang emphasizes that she is not an enslaved person, but Hartley shows the reader that Ang is incorrect in her assertion, that she refuses to accept her reality as her perspective is skewed due to the memories of others in her community. In Bar-Selehm, the White characters retain the wealth and the highest societal positioning. Next, the Mahweni have either been integrated into Bar-Selehm society and work in the service industry, or they remain outside of the city as herders. Finally, there are the Lani—the character of the Other. They reside on the edge of the city in a slum, the Drowning, and are looked down upon by the aforementioned groups. Very few are deemed worthy of respect in Bar-Selehm, one of whom is Ang's oldest sister, Vestris, who only on the surface appears to escape the Drowning and the systemic racism in Bar-Selehm. In his discussion of the novel, Hartley continues:

> I'm under no illusions about the allure of the Victorian past, built as it was on filthy and brutal working conditions, on empire, and on the exploitation of slavery: It was years before I realized that what we knew as the Great Cotton Famine in Lancashire was known in the United States as the American Civil War! Still, I can't help but feel a pang of loss for the extraordinary structures which once defined the region I grew up in, and whose loss signaled decades of hardship and high unemployment. ("A Head for Heights")

By revolving his novel around the subject of memory, that of Ang, her community, and the reader's, Hartley approaches institutional enslavement endeavoring to give biracial people a voice, rather than portraying enslaved people as victims.

Jessica Durgan poses that the neo-Victorian does not revise White British Victorian literature but repeats it, thereby reinforcing colonial systemic racism (214). In her analysis of Gail Carriger's series, Finishing School, Durgan identifies the repeated references to vampirism in the neo-Victorian series stating, "This alternate world depicts British Imperialism as an inhuman (and inhumane) system built on Britain's vampiric ability to prey or feed on their colonies for domestic gain" (216). Hartley describes Ang's societal structure much as Durgan does Carriger's, that a colonialist Bar-Selehm has an underlying racist and repressive structure, one that turns societal members against one another. I do not use the term "citizens" to refer to the people of Bar-Selehm—Ang, the Lani, and the Mahweni—as it denotes recognition of inclusion in the space, and the aforementioned are marginalized. While Durgan identifies "the racial integration policies of the twentieth century" (220) are ingrained within Carriger's series, and it is this that signifies racial discrimination, in Hartley's *Steeplejack*, there is no attempt at or desire for racial integration. As with American enslavement, the enslavers work toward a divisive societal structure, one with an unequal power structure and one that promotes mistrust among the marginalized. When the Beacon, the luxorite stone that gives people in Bar-Selehm light and hope, is stolen, and her apprentice is murdered, it is Ang that investigates. Proactively, the biracial young woman is the hero of the novel, working toward rejecting a segregated societal structure that consumes and objectifies. It is the second-generation memory that aids in the reinforcement of societal constructs; in Lani society, the support for the past comes from the male council and the female midwife, Florihn. Theorist hooks identifies in "An Aesthetics of Blackness" that "Whatever African-Americans created in music, dance, poetry, painting, etc. it was regarded as testimony, bearing witness, challenging racist thinking that suggested that black folks were not fully human, were uncivilized, and that the measure of this was our collective failure to create 'great' art" (*Belonging*, 123). In Ang's society, hooks's observation applies, that people of color, especially the Lani people, who represent biracial people, are thought of by White people as having little worth and, therefore, are unable to contribute to society. This oppressive attitude exists in the past when they were brought to Bar-Selehm and through second-generation memory is reinforced, thereby upholding societal constructs and reinforcing feelings of inferiority.

THE OVERSEER

Ang is a part of the Seventh Street gang and her boss, Morlak, is a character reminiscent of Charles Dickens's Fagin and the later adaptation from Clark of this character in *Black God's Drums*. Decidedly when adding this character type into a neo-slave narrative, this Fagin-like character transforms into the figure of the overseer. Fagin dominates children, subjecting them to physical and mental abuse, brainwashing them into believing that they have no option but to steal for him; the enslaved's overseer torments enslaved people, inflicting violence on African American people of all ages. The overseer appears in the slave narrative as a symbol of unadulterated evil; in slave narratives, there are documented cases of overseers murdering enslaved people. In such cases, the overseers are not prosecuted for the murders as the enslaved are classified as property during the American antebellum period. The figure of the overseer's meaningful inclusion in Hartley's novel contributes to the reader's comprehension of the overwhelming objectification and marginalization that Ang experiences in her society.

ADULTS: THE SUBSTITUTE PARENT

Throughout the novel, Ang emphasizes the void in her life, the emptiness that she feels after the death of her father. Trites identifies the alterations to children's literature as a result of feminism: "Protagonists in novels influenced by feminism . . . have slowly evolved an ability to think about their place in the community without becoming so community-oriented that they become self-effacing. The feminist protagonist cares about other people. But she cares about herself, too" (*Waking*, ix). Ang's missing parents and the concentration on her two sisters and other adults in her life is striking. Trites and other adolescent literature theorists have observed that the initial novel in the young adult trilogy is categorically the bildungsroman. Hartley's *Steeplejack* begins with Ang, who has been forcefully separated from her parents—her father dies in a mining accident, one channeling the colonial abuses in this industry. Even though Ang has her sisters, she is ostensibly alone, living on the fringe of both Lani and Bar-Selehm's White society. Although Trites is discussing White protagonists, her concept of the feminist protagonist applies to the construction of Ang—to an extent. In the slave narrative, enslaved people worked to create a community even though they were forcefully kept from doing so. The trauma experienced devastates the enslaved person's ability to trust. In order for the enslaved person to survive once escaping the space of enslavement, faith in another person must be had, namely abolitionists, other enslaved people, and free African American people. As shown by Trites (*Waking*, ix), the female adolescent protagonist must carve out her own path in life, must fulfill her own needs, but as with the neo-slave narrative, she must also retain the bonds with her community. It is this community, one traumatized by colonialism, that Ang constantly relives via second-generation memory.

MEMORIES AND MOTHERS: FAMILIAL STRUCTURE

A shared history binds most African Americans together, so it stands to reason that like survivors of the Holocaust and 9/11 as theorized by Ulanowicz, second-generational memory impacts the people connected to America's act of enslavement on its own soil. Further, in her analysis of two texts, one from Judy Blume and one from *Zlata Filipović*, Ulanowicz identifies the female protagonists' lives are heavily influenced by the experiences of others, that "second-generation memory is as much shaped by an individual's consciousness of her own immediate circumstances and subject position as it is by stories and artifacts from her elders' past" (13). When the plot begins, Ang is literally and figuratively positioned above Bar-Selehm. She is depicted on the rooftops looking down on the city; she does not exist within the city nor the Lani space of the Drowning. As Ang describes her position, her fellow gang members, and her Lani family and community in the Drowning, Ang's liminality becomes apparent; although she mentors the young Berrit and continues to look out for him throughout the novel, her own state is uncertain. When Ang is introduced, she is conspicuously alone. Her first-person narration of events evokes the slave narrative structure. Ang surveys the city, citing the colonial, race-based political structure that exists in Bar-Selehm, one that continues to be reinforced via second-generation memory. Journalist Don Lemon investigates symbols of the American Civil War, specifically concentrating on those that evoke American enslavement. Lemon states, "The mythology of White supremacy rode into the South on bronze horses during Reconstruction, but let's not pretend folks up North ignored the hoofbeats" and "Mythology is the modus of that inculcation, satisfying our need for stories that sedate the conscience, setting up patterns whereby we deconstruct and justify circumstances as needed" (104–5). In Hartley's novel, the stolen Beacon is a constant symbol of colonization, a light that exists as a daily reminder to the people of Bar-Selehm and surrounding areas that there is an uneven power structure based in racism and continuous reinforcement.

Ang realizes while she is on top of a building that the Beacon, the image of immense wealth and the constant reminder of the class system in place, has gone missing. The monument to racism, as Lemon has stated, is replicated by Hartley: Ang highlights the immense monetary value of the piece of luxorite and implies that the politicians have audacity for placing it where the marginalized and the poverty-stricken will see it every day and night because, after all, it glows. Pondering the removal of the Beacon and her space in the societal hierarchy, Ang thinks:

> It was gone, and with that, the world had shifted on its axis, a minute adjustment that altered everything. Even for someone like me, who was used to standing tall in dangerous places, the thought was unsettling. The Beacon was a constant, a part of the world that was just simply there. That it wasn't felt ominous. But it also felt right, as if the day should be commemorated with darkness. (Hartley *Steeplejack*, 6–7)

Second-generation memory comes into play here, as not only is the Beacon a reminder of colonialism and Ang's enslavement, but it also reinforces the fact that the system in place forces the Lani to reside in the Drowning, causing their poverty and, subsequently, Ang's father's death. The death of Ang's father and her memories of him are intermingled with her search for the stolen Beacon, once she is kidnapped and subsequently hired by Josiah Willinghouse, a Lani member of parliament, specifically the opposition. In *The Guardian* (2018), Ang discovers that Willinghouse's father had a disregard for the miners' lives, failing to secure the required safety protocols, an act that leads to the death of Ang's father in a mine collapse. The commentary about the class system becomes apparent, with some of the Lani people being used and discarded by those with wealth and clout.

In addition, the misogynistic traits of Bar-Selehm reverberate, objectifying Ang further as her memories of her father reinforce. When Ang returns to the Drowning for the birth of her sister Rahvey's child, the agency she feels on top of the buildings, the independence, is fleeting and is replaced with oppression. The midwife, Florihn, reinforces the lack of worth that Lani girls and women hold in Lani society, one that Ang observes is male led. Each time Ang asserts her power, thereby acting as a hero to those around her, Florihn reinforces the second-generation memory: "This is our way. The Lani way," crushing Ang's desire for change (Hartley *Steeplejack*, 30). It is not until Ang discovers her sister Vestris's role in stealing the Beacon and returns the monument to Bar-Selehm does she go back to the Drowning, trying to change the gender-based hierarchy in place. As Trites offers, "To refer to someone's 'subject position(s)' is to acknowledge simultaneously her dependence on language structures and her point of view within the matrices of her subjectivity" (*Waking* 28). Although Ang works to change how third and fourth daughters are treated in Lani society, she is still told by Rahvey that she no longer belongs in the Lani community. Her act of saving the Beacon is recognized by Bar-Selehm society; however, Ang's heroism is diminished by the skewing of the part that Ang takes. In the next two novels in the series, *Firebrand* (2017) and *The Guardian*, Ang's subjectivity fluctuates, as her acts of heroism are purposefully concealed by Willinghouse, who informs Ang that she has more power to enact change as a secret agent for civil rights. In *Steeplejack*, Ang is shown as a hero for the voiceless; and some of the boys are marginalized.

The prominence of the African American female mother character has been well documented by theorists. In *Saints, Sinners, Saviors: Strong Black Women in African American Literature*, Harris highlights the stereotypical representations of the African American mother figure in 1970s and 1980s television, citing the physically large and nurturing "Mammy" caricature as a dominant character in twentieth-century television; even though this character was prominent, Harris states that another character also existed. Harris delineates the self-sacrificing mother figure, one who relinquishes everything for the sake of her community, further warning that this character is, too, a stereotype. When Hartley's novel opens, Ang is working and mulling over the behavior of her new apprentice, a thirteen-year-old Lani male by the name of Berrit. While Ang's positioning in her society as Other constricts her movement and behavior, she deftly finds ways to obtain her freedom from constraint albeit only temporarily. It is Ang that narrates the novel. By having Ang tell her own story so that Bar-Selehm societal guidelines are envisioned from her point of view, Hartley ensures that Ang has some power—it is she that asserts authority over the narrative. Next, when the reader first encounters Ang, she is taking control of an uncontrollable situation. She immediately contemplates the death of Berrit, without naming him or giving exact details, but quickly ventures away from the topic due to its dangerous nature—those distracted in her position, which is physically on the top of a building, face certain death. Ang consciously tenses her body, realizing, "If I relaxed even fractionally, I would die on the cobbles eighty feet below" (Hartley, *Steeplejack*). Unlike the stereotypical mother figures that Harris discusses, Ang is by herself and does not appear to have any form of community. As she maneuvers to complete her work, after noting her superiority in the field, Ang reaches a location where another chimney sweep has died previously and matter-of-factly reveals that when young, the gender identity of the steeplejack is irrelevant, but once they reach adolescence, steeplejacks are mainly cisgender males because "no one is looking for a bride that can outlift him" (Hartley, *Steeplejack*). After this assertion, Ang reaffirms her desire to remain alone in this space, also proclaiming that this is her reason for becoming a steeplejack in the first place rather than her proficiency in her craft. According to Ang, "I liked it up here by myself, high above the world: no Morlak looking over my shoulder, no boys testing how far they had to go before I threw a punch, no wealthy white folk curling their lips as if I put them off their breakfast" (Hartley, *Steeplejack*). Ang comes close to becoming what Harris terms the "superhuman Black woman," which is concerning: this character has no equal and, as a result, remains alone (174).

Harris warns against this character and the self-sacrificing mother, one who places her group association, whether it be children or, in the case of the slave narrative, the enslaved community, above her own needs. When documenting the various familial structures offered in Disney films, Lynne Lundquist and Gary Westfahl highlight the surrogate parent figure, observing what they call the "mentor character," who ultimately acts as a guide, briefly, before being displaced by the child (164). The theorists document "a role reversal: although animals and magical adults first appear in parental roles, the children later assume the parental roles, with the animals and the adults recast as their children. In effect, children manage to construct their own families, with themselves as parents" (164). As the novel begins, Ang immediately informs her reader of her age, seventeen, thereby marking her as a character in transition from adolescent to adult. While Ang asserts her independence and her momentary freedom, she also displays her desire to belong to a community. As Ang describes her one moment that lacks outside restraint, her movement on top of the buildings, she continuously reflects on the Seventh Street gang and what life is like in Bar-Selehm for each of the three groups. Looking over the city, Ang is unable to escape the societal hierarchy and her place within. Once she discovers the theft of the Beacon—Hartley frames his coming-of-age neo-slave narrative within a mystery that could lead to a war—she meets with Tanish, who informs her of her sister Rahvey's impending delivery of her child. Once they discover Berrit's body and subsequently Rahvey's daughter is born (the daughter that Ang must adopt because the child is considered the cursed third daughter, just like Ang, and will be disposed of if not), Ang is launched into the role of caregiver. Throughout the text Ang describes

Tanish as a child rather than a person in a liminal adolescent state: to Ang, he is someone who needs to be protected. Ang desires to shield Tanish from this traumatic experience—she has seen death prior to that of Berrit—in order to allow him what childhood, what innocence he has left to remain intact. After locating the body in the alley, Ang takes control of the situation and sends Tanish to obtain assistance. Trites documents that adolescents in their liminal state are both powerful and "disempowered" (*Disturbing the Universe* ix). With regard to the former, Trites states that in one such instance they become so "in the typical scenario of teenagers succeeding in their rebellions against authority figures" and the latter "in the increased objectification of the teenage body that leads many adolescents to perpetrate acts of violence against the Self or Other" (ix). After she takes charge and sends Tanish away, Ang has a moment to herself when she can mourn, removing the copper pendant from Berrit's neck in order to later give it to a family member in remembrance. Ang comprehends the correct way to act in this situation, to preserve the jewelry for some who "had loved him" (Hartley); unbeknown to Ang, that person is Ang herself rather than his grandmother, who sold him to the gang. Ang becomes the adult figure in both children's life—she names Kalla, a symbolic act in Lani society, takes care of Tanish, and works to solve the murder of Berrit.

CONCLUSION: PROBLEMATIC ANTIFEMINIST ATTRIBUTES OF THE NOVEL

While waiting for Berrit to arrive, Tanish discovers his corpse. When Ang examines Berrit's body, she becomes aware that the death was not accidental, but rather Berrit has been murdered. Ang takes the time to ponder her regrets, namely that she did not spend enough time with Berrit before his death. She states that she wanted to speak to Berrit, he is approximately ten years old before his death, but that she has been called away before she could do so: she did not want to attempt to make him more comfortable with Morlak in full view. Ang identifies that Morlak has been sexually harassing her, continuing his predatory behavior when he tries to rape her. Morlak is not brought to justice for his attempted rape but, instead, for his part in the plot to steal the Beacon.

By joining with Willinghouse and utilizing his wealth and clout in Bar-Selehm, Ang is successfully able to displace the adults—Morlak, Vestris, and Stefan Von Strahden—thereby forming her own community and ostensibly becoming an authority figure. The issue is that the disempowerment that Trites documents in *Disturbing the Universe* comes first. Willinghouse has Ang forcefully taken to his home, where he offers her a job so she may discover the murderer of Berrit and the thief of the Beacon, while also stopping a war between the factions before it begins. Willinghouse has called upon her because "You are, I am told, the finest steeplejack in the city" (Hartley, *Steeplejack*). He places her in danger, almost getting Ang killed, because she is the object that can return the Beacon to its rightful place, thereby unifying the factions. While Ang is in his presence, she even reveals that he makes her "feel young and vulnerable in ways I had not felt in years" (Hartley).

More problematic is the fact that Willinghouse is Lani, male, and older than Ang, and he is featured as if he is to be her love interest in subsequent novels in the trilogy. A member of the Lani community that preys upon Ang, Willinghouse continues throughout the trilogy to employ Ang allegedly for the good of Bar-Selehm, when in fact it is for his own political gain. He goes as far as referring to Ang as Morlak's "slave" (Hartley). It is unsettling for the reader to encounter these antifeminist attributes in *Steeplejack*. It is on account of the #MeToo Movement that unequal power relationships have been exposed in Hollywood, leading to many women voicing how they have been preyed upon by men in supervisory roles. While Willinghouse is jailed in *The Guardian*, he never really loses: the power and position remain. He does, however, fail to secure Ang's loyalty any further. In a plot point that is underdeveloped, appearing at the end of the third novel, is the lesbian relationship between Ang and Willinghouse's sister, Dahria. While the attempt at inclusivity is appreciated, the lack of development is not and emerges as tokenism.

In order to assert her power in the novel, Ang must risk her life and solve the murder of Berrit, displacing the postcolonial societal guidelines; further, she must form the community, the family that she lost upon the death of her beloved father. She must alter the societal guidelines in the Lani community that make her the cursed third daughter and that place Rahvey's daughter in a life-threatening position. Ang exposes Vestris for her part in the murder, returns the Beacon to its place in Bar-Selehm, and assists in altering Lani societal guidelines, thereby allowing Rahvey to raise her third daughter; by doing so, Ang transitions from adolescent to adult. However, with all of Ang's heroic acts, she remains marginalized in Lani society.

Chapter 5

SELF-IMAGE AND NARRATION IN THE YOUNG ADULT STEAMPUNK NOVELS *THE BLACK GOD'S DRUMS* AND THE DREAD NATION SERIES

INTRODUCTION: THE FEMALE STORYTELLER TRADITION

In the young adult steampunk novels *The Black God's Drums* (*BGD*; 2018) and *Dread Nation* (*DN*; 2018), authors P. Djèlí Clark and Justina Ireland offer readers a new wave of female protagonists leading the neo-slave narrative. Detrimentally, many twenty-first-century young adult novels featuring African American female protagonists portray these young women as weak and unable to care for themselves. As I have shown in previous chapters and publications with regard to the neo-slave narrative, the African American female protagonists are a re-creation of constructs created and reinforced in American enslavement era texts. Regarding the neo-slave narratives that kickstarted the genre—those literary contributions were written for adults featuring adult characters—many may also be placed in the alternative history genre. The fantastical qualities of some of the neo-slave narratives (e.g., Beloved's ghost haunting Sethe in Morrison's *Beloved*, Dana's time travel in Butler's *Kindred*, or Ishmael Reed's postmodernist construction of time in *Flight to Canada*) enable Black writers authorial license to wrest back control of the enslaved person's story while also coming to terms with the trauma experienced due to enslavement.

Further, the rewriting of American history namely the Civil War as contained within some neo-slave narratives (see those examined in this chapter) should enable contemporary authors to revise history from a more advantageous standpoint, one that is no longer idealistic but rather authentic in its portrayal. In reference to idealism, to what is being referred in the case of the slave narratives is the portrait of the enslaved person; so that the antebellum reader vies for the enslaved, the image of the enslaved person must be one without flaw, one that elicits sympathy, or else the emotional connection will be shattered and the narrative unsuccessful in its purpose. Fantastical elements, such as Ireland's zombie hordes, are representative, meant not to distract but enhance the reader's comprehension of the American antebellum South and its inhuman societal practices. In his study of African American trauma stemming from enslavement, Ron Eyerman identifies that "The trauma of forced servitude and of nearly complete subordination to the will and whims of another was thus not necessarily something directly experienced by many of the subjects of this study, but came to be central to their attempts to forge a collective identity out of its remembrance" (1). Eyerman's study is that of the postbellum African American text and the experiences that are reflected as a result of the collective memory of trauma. For the neo-slave narrative, so that the generic contributions may be considered as such and so that writers may offer a new generation of readers reflections regarding collective trauma, neo-slave narratives require adaptation of source material.

The objective of this chapter is to examine the adaptations made to the narrative, specifically to the voice that tells readers the story. Meghann Meeusen analyzes adaptations of children's literature, highlighting the possibilities that cinematic adaptations offer in reference to the binary of good versus evil. Meeusen, in reference to the cinematic adaptation of *Tales of Deveraux*, documents the intensity with which "the message of the film" alters the portrayal of the binary and offers the improvements enabled by the visual medium (4). Valerie Smith in her nominal essay about neo-slave narratives contends that the neo-slave narrative comprises not only works reenvisioning the horrors of slavery but also those set since Reconstruction ("Neo-Slave Narratives" 168). Smith's observations are key to the understanding of the placement of these more recent novels and novellas in the slave narrative genre as they are not as overt in their construction as reflecting the past enslavement of the peoples of Africa. Smith discusses narrative structure, stating, "They approach the institution of slavery from a myriad of perspectives and embrace a variety of styles of writing: from realist novels grounded in historical research to speculative fiction, postmodern experiments, satire, and works that combine these diverse models" (168). Tellingly, speculative fiction has been included in Smith's list; however, this categorization with regard to the slave narrative tends to be constituted from Morrison's and Butler's offerings in critical outputs.

It is the contributions about African American adolescent women in the early twenty-first century that have made a significant impact on the genre, but not consistently in a positive way. Afrofuturism was created as a method of making sure that Black persons were both included in science fiction outputs and at the forefronts of proposed futures. In one of the earliest Afrofuturistic writings, "The Comet" (1920), Du Bois adapts the Adam and Eve story, refreshing the plot and making it about the last people on Earth instead of the first. Du Bois, who has been heralded for his contributions to African American literature and the Harlem Renaissance, was misogynistic and classist. His desire for racial uplift was commendable, except that it led to the attempted silencing of Hurston and her feminist publications, namely *Their Eyes Were Watching God* (1937). This foray into previous African American literature has not been done in order to suggest that literary contributions from and about African Americans must be written to meet Du Bois's standards—far from it. First, Du Bois has been referenced here to document his contribution to the Afrofuturism (speculative fiction) genre. Second, his short story addition to the dystopic genre places an African American man in the lead, while reflecting the inequality of American society in the early twentieth century, implying that discriminatory practices will continue into the future. Finally, Du Bois and his Harlem Renaissance followers did a great disservice not only to Hurston as a writer but to literature as a whole when he devalued her work. Hurston's *Their Eyes* gave readers a strong, forward-thinking woman in the character of Janie, one that returns home and tells her story to her friend, Pheoby. As a classically trained anthropologist who studied under Franz Boas at Barnard College, Hurston thoroughly documented oral traditions in African American communities, traditions that she has incorporated into her construction of Janie. It is Janie that returns home, barefoot, clad in overalls, and hair in braids, taking the long walk through town past the gossips and toward her friend. DoVeanna S. Fulton contends that in Hurston's novel, the character of Nanny carries on "the tradition of the African griot," the storyteller figure (as well as one "derived ... from antiliteracy and pro-Christian slave policy") but that there is an "absence of publicly sanctioned space and limited methods available for Black women to relate their history" (1). In other words, this is why Nanny, Janie's grandmother, is deprived of the pulpit, thereby acting in the role of preacher (a traditionally male one) without societal approval. After Janie comes home, she sits outside, telling her story to her friend out on her porch, a conventional meeting place for African American men, as witnessed in the novel after Janie's second marriage. Unlike Du Bois's desire for a sanitized image of African American women (he heralded Jessie Redmon Fauset's *There Is Confusion* [1924] as an ideal racial uplift novel), Hurston offers reader a positive construction of a female character, one who not only survives abuse but is also content with her identity. She returns self-assured, and her lack of shame shocks the townsfolk. Hurston gives to readers a woman confident in who she is, offering to her female audience an unabashed history of a female-positive woman. As is consistent with many of the other selections studied for this book, both Clark and Ireland continue the female storyteller tradition in their respective publications.

Clark gives readers Creeper (also known as Jacqueline), an adolescent African American female residing on her own in the midst of Free New Orleans. For the novella, Clark has created an alternative history text: it is in New Orleans that the end to enslavement comes due to the enslaved revolting. Creeper discovers a plot by Confederate soldiers to obtain orisha[1] Shango's thunder so that they may reignite the Civil War. Clark provides readers with a story in which a group of women—adolescent and adult—stop a war, save the city of New Orleans, and abolish enslavement for good. Like Clark, Maryland native Ireland rewrites the Civil War; however, in her case the war has been placed on hold due to the zombification of the Gettysburg soldiers. Jane McKeene, also known as the Angel of the Crossroads because she saves travelers from being bitten by zombies, is forcefully sent to Baltimore for training at Miss Preston's School of Combat. African American girls are not permitted to remain with their families; they are taken against their will to a school to be taught how to be Attendants for wealthy Caucasian women. Jane tells the reader that "An Attendant's job is simple: keep her charge from being killed by the dead, and her virtue from being compromised by potential suitors. It is a task easier said than done" (*DN* 10). The enforced removal of African American children from their families has been regularly documented in slave narratives, Ireland replicating the trauma that enslaved parents faced in her second novel in the series. Ireland, however, also reveals the child's feelings toward forced separation in *DN*, as Jane's confusion and anguish are recorded in her letters to her mother. In addition, Jane has a companion, Katherine Deveraux, one she does not consider a friend until the second novel, *Deathless Divide*. Like Jane, Katherine has secrets connected to her racial identity and antebellum societal construction. Katherine, who becomes one of two protagonists in the alternating narrative structure in *Deathless Divide*, is the biracial daughter of a Louisiana sex worker, who hides her past behind lies she tells to the other young women at the school. Through Jane's insensitive comments about Katherine—"Katherine is passing light; a body likely wouldn't even know that she was colored unless someone told them" (*DN* 13)—the reader encounters the challenges that biracial young women would have faced, specifically the marginalization by both Black and White persons. While Katherine in the initial novel appears as the guide character to Jane (the sidekick), she emerges in the sequel as a developed character, one that spends the plot establishing her identity and coming to terms with her need for human companionship.

Underlying the action-filled plots is an African American adolescent girl's coming-of-age story. It is integral to this study that the reader comprehends that (a) White female adolescents' stories are primarily examined in textual analyses even in the twenty-first century, and (b) African American and White girls have different experiences during childhood and adolescence. While there are some commonalities in experiences, we as academics should not place all adolescent girls into the same group, assuming that all of their experiences are alike.

In both Clark's *BGD* and Ireland's *DN* and *Deathless Divide* (2020), the female protagonists come to terms with their respective identities: who they believe they are supposed to be (unimportant to the societal structure) and who they are in reality (heroes). Society at large does not take these characters seriously. Their reasoning ranges from the norm in YA literature—adults who disbelieve the abilities of an adolescent—to misogyny and racism. Creeper, Jane, and Katherine are regarded as trivial because of their age, gender, and race. Further, this study will investigate the need that Creeper, Jane, and Katharine have for their communities, which aid in their acceptance of their true selves and their personal growth. Throughout childhood and adolescence, many African American girls and young women are repeatedly confronted by negative imagery about Black women, much of which stems from antebellum America. Even though Clark and Ireland include constructs regarding the female enslaved person in reference to their female protagonists in their works, they ultimately revise the protagonists creating independent, heroic African American female characters. By doing so, the authors refute stereotypes, thereby asserting positive images about African American young women; they tear down those that continue to persist into the twenty-first century, damaging African American young women's self-image and corrupting society.

FOSTER'S LAYOUT OF THE SLAVE NARRATIVE: THE NARRATIVE'S VOICE

Eminent theorist Frances Smith Foster documents the structure of the slave narrative, noting the Judeo-Christian mythological similarities in the texts as intentional (84). As Foster breaks down the slave narrative's construction, the narrative's writer is intentionally not identified by the theorist, yet the protagonist of the narrative—the enslaved person—is. As has been well documented by theorists, the voices of the enslaved tended to be documented by the Caucasian, abolitionist writer; this happened because formerly enslaved people were largely unable to read and write, so the term "writer" literally refers to the person who wrote the narrative down. By omitting references to the Caucasian writer from her chapter "The Plot of Antebellum Slave Narratives," thereby discussing the enslaved person's voice and the Judeo-Christian influences on the narrative's structure, it appears that Foster removes the editorial voice that may have made alterations to the narrative plot; the writer may have changed the narrative in order to further the agenda of the writer themselves, of the abolitionist movement, and/or of societal construct reinforcement. At first glance, the writer's agenda may have an abolitionist scope, ultimately equality may not be its motivator and rather reinforcement of the hierarchical structure in place may be of interest to the Caucasian writer. Recently, historians are calling attention to the fact that abolitionists may have desired freedom from enslavement for enslaved people, but that does not necessarily mean that Caucasian people wanted American societal equality. Connolly examines antebellum children's literature, observing that during this period the texts taught behavior modification for children (3). She also states that some writers imparted information about social outreach to the poverty stricken as well as "admonitions for personal responsibility" (3). Connolly's description of the messages included within antebellum children's literature relate how influential the adult voice sees itself and, if an inappropriate (and racist) message is sent, how societal change may be wrought. Theorizing about the audience, Connolly writes, "Yet, for all the suggested radical nature of literature which encouraged children's engagement in social reform, the vision of the child as hope for the nation's future was often a circumscribed one, largely offered by a white, middle-class authors to white-middle-class children as a way to ensure a relatively comparable future" (3). The primacy of White children as the audience shows their subjectivity in the antebellum period, whereas children of color, specifically those who are enslaved, are either objectified, villainized, or absent from the reader's view.

By reenvisioning the neo-slave narrative as one for an adolescent readership, and one in the twenty-first century where diversity, inclusivity, and equity are heralded, writers have the opportunity to center their creations on African American and biracial young women. These women are heroic yet flawed, making their characterization relatable for their readership. The formerly enslaved are idealized in the retelling of their stories, an act meant to create believability for the White reader. Due to prejudices regarding race, gender, and enslaved people, there was bias from readers when approaching the narrative. Idealization works to place the slave narrative into the popular genre of sentimental literature (as theorists have stated), done so to elicit sympathy from the reader. By categorizing the slave narrative as sentimental literature, readers and reviewers work to discount the reality that enslaved people faced, particularly for women.

Foster works to give control of the formerly enslaved person's story to the person who is the supposed subject of the narrative. In her book, prior to the aforementioned chapter, Foster acknowledges the obstacles placed in the path of the formerly enslaved narrator, namely the discriminatory attitudes of readers and stereotypical constructs regarding African Americans (65). According to Foster, "Both the literary and social histories of their audience, which was predominantly White middle class and of their authors, who were black and socially subordinate to their readers, determined the climate, models, and expectations that significantly determined the content and form of the writing" (65). While the formerly enslaved person—the inhumane treatment of and trauma experienced by—should be the primary concentrations of the narrative, Foster observes the deliberate subjugation of the protagonist's voice in favor of the needs of the readers. As Foster asserts with regard to the treatment of the formerly enslaved in connection to the societal hierarchal construct and that of the narrative: "The success of his [the slave's] narrative required that he be perceived as an example, but economic and often personal success required that he be seen as an exemplar" (65). In effect, the enslaved person who ought to be the focal point of their story thereby becomes an idealized victim for the northern audience. Once this is achieved, the slave is then transformed into an activist upon whom the narrative itself and genre of the slave narrative rely. Foster continues, "The struggle to maintain a balance between self and the world, the subjective and the objective, which is waged by most but achieved by few autobiographical writers, became more significant for the slave narrator" (65).

The neo-slave narrative emerged resulting from an effort to recast the enslaved's story. By utilizing the narrative as a basis for a new and powerful genre, Black writers attempt to remove the enslaved from the marginalized state that has been forced upon them during their portrayal in the slave narrative. The purpose for skewing the image of the enslaved in the original genre was the gaining of sympathy, of empathy from a Caucasian northern audience, thereby ensuring the audience's acceptance of the narrative. As a result of this recasting of the formerly enslaved person's story, the narrator is once again exploited by the system, but in this case the subject is in partial control of the narrative. As with movements, there are those who are cast as figureheads, sacrificing their personal needs and desires for the movement. As readers, we must be careful to examine all facets of the slave narrative and we must be mindful that ultimately the motivation for the genre was not autobiographical, historical, or adventure but was to abolish enslavement therefore saving African American people's lives. On the one hand, formerly enslaved people relinquished their stories only to have them commandeered by others for societal exclusion; on the other hand, individuality is abandoned for the greater good—the freedom of the four million enslaved people.

THE NEO-SLAVE NARRATIVE: OCTAVIA E. BUTLER'S *KINDRED*

While there is debate as to the initial contribution to the neo-slave narrative genre, consensus offers Butler's *Kindred* (1979) and Gayl Jones's *Corregidora* (1975) at the forefront of not only the genre as a whole but also in contributions from and about African American women. Butler's impact on twenty-first-century additions to the literature is most notable when examining young adult dystopian fiction. Nadine Flagel highlights temporal dislocation as the tool through which Butler bypasses any disconnect that the narrator—Dana—may experience when attempting to identify with the members of her family who were enslaved in Maryland during the antebellum period (218). Flagel continues, "Through the insertion of slave narrative elements, Dana's otherwise fantastic experience with slavery becomes typical, credible" (218). In *Kindred*, Dana travels in time so she may meet and comprehend her family's connection to the antebellum period, namely that her progenitors are an enslaved woman and a male enslaver. Flagel asserts that attributes of the slave narrative's plot have been added to Butler's novel in order to add plausibility to a novel that has a protagonist travel to the past so that she may meet her grandmother, Alice, and her grandfather, Rufus. Further, Flagel offers that Butler's novel emphasizes the enslaved woman's experience, calling attention to the frequent threats of physical assault and sexual violation (218).

As Butler's Dana traverses time, she comes to the realization that she cannot alter events without risking her own future and that of her family. Dana's familial line is descended from a child who is the product of rape. The "typicality" of which Flagel writes refers to the fact that bodily violation for African American women was commonplace during the period of American enslavement. Even though Dana knows that she can stop Alice's rape, she also understands that she must accept the violation of her family in order for her to exist in her time. As Foster posits, "From Clotel to Kizzy, our most frequent images of slave women are as victims of illicit sexual intercourse and as childless mothers" (xxix). Regarding *Kindred* and the character of Dana, both of Foster's observations may be applied; it is Dana's grandmother that is sexually exploited and Dana who is childless. In Foster's case, "childless" refers to enslaved women who have had their children stolen from them and sold away. Dana appears as both victim and victimized as she is implicit in the violation (she stands by and allows its occurrence) but also is powerless to cease it, as she will irrevocably damage her family if she does so. Butler posits the ethical dilemma that Dana faces, namely, that if Dana stops the sexual assault from happening, she will not be born.

Butler's early neo-slave narrative shines in its brilliance as she gets the crux of one of the problems with the slave narrative, namely the portrayal of enslaved or formerly enslaved women. Because the slave narrative tends to be told by male writers, the representation of African American women is questionable, as they are either categorized as victims of physical and/or sexual abuse or as the wounded mother; as a result, enslaved women become idealized by male writers—they are symbolically "saved." They are no longer individual women but rather representational constructs regarding the Black female body. Lynn Orilla Scott affirms, "While enslaved women are portrayed as passive victims of sexual exploitation in narratives written by men, women narrators portray themselves as active and heroic agents in the struggle for freedom" (Scott). Integrally, the agency of the enslaved woman is the primary aspect that is embraced by young adult neo-slave writers. The antebellum South's constructs regarding African American women breaks enslaved women down into parts. The reenvisioning of the enslaved women in the neo-slave narrative reveals to readers the entire enslaved woman: a strong, flawed, realistic woman is shown instead of one who has been reimagined—idealized—for others' purposes. The young adult neo-slave narrative written about Black young women gives writers the opportunity to convey these characters' points of view, voices that were traditionally in the background of slave narratives.

In reference to the adult neo-slave narrative, by recasting the slave narrative, overlaying its construction on the Black Arts science fictional novel, Butler places *Kindred*'s Dana at the forefront of the plot, giving her a certain amount of control in the text. Butler neither victimizes nor sexualizes Dana, allowing her to act as a witness to events that had unfolded long before her time. Dana must explore her familial background, an act that enables her to emotionally connect with her past and deal with the trauma that results. When Dana loses an arm, Butler symbolically chips away at the female body, offering Dana as more than a collection of body parts. Dana is more than only a body: when enslavers sold enslaved women, it was the body in which they had interest, not the woman's mind or emotions. While Dana is aware of what happened to her ancestors in the past, any illusions that she may have had about being able to change events are symbolically left in the past with Dana's arm. Further, Butler enables Dana to become the narrator, giving her a voice that she may not otherwise have had. With Creeper, Clark regains control of the slave narrative and through the neo-slave narrative attempts to continue in the tradition of Butler, thereby endeavoring to alter preconceived notions about the Black female body.

CLARK'S CREEPER AND HER CHILDHOOD

In *The Black God's Drums,* Clark places the slave narrative construction over that of the young adult twenty-first-century dystopian novella. As customary with the slave narrative, immediately upon opening, Creeper offers as much knowledge as she has about the circumstances surrounding her birth. Imogen Russell Williams for the UK's *Guardian* questions whether the YA genre is such or whether it exists only as a marketing gimmick; she subsequently defines the YA genre as "more likely [than the teen genre] to deal frankly with sex, tackle challenging issues and adult relationships, and feature swearing." According to Williams, the "teen genre," which is designed for twelve- to fourteen-year-old readers, tends to concentrate on "violence" rather than the aforementioned. In examining Clark's novella, Williams's assertions are accurate if not simplistic in their presentation. Creeper is introduced as a thirteen-year-old African American female who has a spiritual connection with the African goddess of "the storms," Oya. As Clark's novella may also be considered to be part of the neo-Victorian genre, Clark alludes to Creeper's life as being like that of Oliver Twist (there are references to workhouses and Fagin-like characters). Following the traditional slave narrative format, it is Creeper who acts as narrator, thereby taking control of her story. Foster deconstructs the slave narrative structure, stating that the enslaved person's childhood is condensed and that "from the beginning, slave narrators had started chronologically with birth and childhood and thus began their narratives with an exposition of life as an innocent" (92). Foster refers to the lack of knowledge that the children have regarding their enslaved state. Creeper's childhood is short, comprising memories of her *maman* recounting her birth in a storm and comments from Creeper that allude to her mother's death. For Creeper, innocence is short-lived due to her mother's death from yellow fever and her subsequent orphaned state. As the novella opens, Creeper's physicality is in the forefront; the protagonist reveals that she is small in stature and fast, both of which enable her to quickly evade the police and those that would place her either in an orphanage or in a workhouse that employs children. Creeper includes herself in the community of the children she calls the street rats, yet she is shown alone often throughout the novella. Foster observes that it was for a brief moment that enslaved children lived ignorant of their confinement, that it was done by the writer on purpose in order to emphasize the enslaved person's shock and disgust at learning of the reality of life for a person of African descent in the South (96). When the reader is introduced to Creeper, she waxes poetic about New Orleans and then she is elucidating the benefits of living in Le Grand Murs, namely its ability to offer a safe place to sleep. Because Creeper is small, she can cram herself into a cubbyhole and watch the airships from an advantageous position. The physicality of Creeper is significant in reference to the slave narrative and the portrayal of children. In a slave narrative, the formerly enslaved person's voice manages the story; however, it is an adult that reflects about the past, one that includes their childhood. Like women in male-centric narratives, children take a secondary role in the narrative. The reader must be mindful that adolescence is not portrayed, is not thought of in the nineteenth century as we do currently. For example, Douglass experiences severe abuse once he reaches the age of sixteen; at this point he has reached adulthood and is forced to work in the fields doing heavy labor. For Jacobs, "the influences of slavery had had the same effect on me that they had on other young girls; they had made me prematurely knowing, concerning the evil ways of the world. I know what I did, and I did it with deliberate calculation." What Jacobs refers to is sex, specifically the fear of violation of her body by an enslaver and the great lengths she takes to save herself from rape. In Clark's novella, Creeper is thirteen, and she alludes to dressing as a boy to disguise herself from sexual assault. Her fear is close to fruition once she arrives at the brothel.

Channeling the nineteenth-century adventure story, Clark has Creeper dream of leaving New Orleans and traveling around the world as a member of an airship's crew. This innocence is shattered once she overhears the Confederate soldiers talking about a Haitian scientist who is in control of a weapon known as the Black god's drums or Shango's thunder. Creeper, who admits to stealing in order to support herself (an aspect of life documented in the slave narrative), realizes the importance of the information she has overheard and sees it as her ticket on board an airship. Over the course of two days, Creeper contemplates how to best use the information for the highest yield, not considering how detrimental the Black god's drums could be to her community. The issue is that even though Creeper sees herself as part of New Orleans, this is after all an adolescent narrator and her vision is often shortsighted, so no attempt is offered to give this information to an adult. Also, if Clark's novella is to be envisioned as a neo-slave narrative, the reader must be cognizant of the fact that for enslaved people, in many cases they were unable to trust their community due to the fear that enslavers forced upon them. Enslaved people many times could not trust other enslaved people because of the possibility that they would be turned in to the enslavers, to the authorities, an act that could mean death. Creeper is alone and is wary of interactions with adults. In fact, as Creeper traverses the city on her way to Madamesville, New Orleans' red light district, the protagonist reports that there are no responsible adults but rather those concerned with Mardi Gras and their personal enjoyment.

Clark places his female characters at the forefront of the novella, and it is the bodies of these adolescent and adult women that are initially on display. Jacobs furthers her enlightening examination regarding the abhorrent behavior of enslavers, seeking understanding as she addresses her White female readers as she does so: "But, O, ye happy women, whose purity has been sheltered from childhood, who have been free to choose the objects of your affection, whose homes are protected by law, do not judge the poor desolate slave girl too severely!" In her narrative, Jacobs documents at length the sexualization of enslaved young women, how the experiences of Black enslaved young women are contrasted with those of White young women. Jacobs hints at the crux of the stereotyping of enslaved Black girls and young women. First, Jacobs reveals that while White girls and young women have their innocence and chastity protected, no such assurances are extended to African American girls and young women. Whereas Foster asserts that enslaved children are briefly unaware of their societal position (92–93)—that they are classified as commodities instead of human beings—Jacobs and Elizabeth Keckley (*Behind the Scenes, or, Thirty Years a Slave, and Four Years in the White House*, 1868) both expose that, as girls, their innocence is lost to a system that forces objectification on them. Keckley tells her readers that at the age of four, she is an enslaved child who is required to take on the task of caring for her female enslaver's infant. When the child falls, Keckley is physically assaulted; the physical abuse toward children by their enslavers is tragically affirmed.

In addition, Jacobs brings to light a startling realization, that innocence about sex for an adolescent young woman is shattered once they reach a certain age. Under the pen name of Brent, Jacobs deconstructs the experiences that enslaved young and older women faced, issues she asserts are not supposed to be brought to light. For example, an enslaved woman is sold by Dr. Flint, and Jacobs describes her forceful removal: "She had forgotten that it was a crime for a slave to tell who was the father of her child" (Jacobs). Sex for female enslaved people is something of shame, fear, and violence. The innocence that is afforded White females regarding their sexuality[2] is constructed out of a societal myth regarding purity and, in order to keep the myth intact, someone is placed in the opposite role, is Othered. According to Robin Bernstein in her examination of Harriet Beecher Stowe's abolitionist serialized novel, "In one of its most important functions, *Uncle Tom's Cabin* installed a black-white logic in American visions of childhood" (15). As is pointed out by theorists including Hazel Carby, White female enslavers were placed in the role of chaste woman while African American enslaved women were cast as overly sexual. In a way, the English Renaissance Madonna/whore dichotomy for women has reared its ugly head once more. Regarding the enslaved woman, Carby explains, "The objective of stereotypes is not to reflect or represent a reality but to function as a disguise, or mystification, of objective social relations" (22). In sum, stereotypes regarding African American enslaved women existed to excuse abusive behavior from the enslavers and to excuse sexual violations. In other words, enslavers create constructs so that they may blame the victim of their rape, one of the worst misogynistic acts that can be enacted. As can be witnessed in literary contributions in the twenty-first century as well as authentic testimonials, many African American girls and young women still suffer the ill effects of enslavement stereotypes. The loss of innocence is a rape in itself: facing stereotypes about African American women and racial discrimination regarding Black people, many girls and young women are deprived of a safe childhood and adolescence.

After overhearing the plot to steal Shango's thunder, Creeper picks some pockets and then goes to the Shá Roux, to Madame Diouf's brothel in what Creeper terms "neutral territory" (*BGD*). This part of New Orleans is a nonsegregated zone, meaning that people of all races are legally permitted to interact—socially or sexually. Clark's terminology here is symbolic, referring to the objectification of the body, the space in which there is a free-for-all toward the female human body. Continuing, Creeper tells the reader that sex workers and their clients are representational of various ethnicities and sexual orientations. As Creeper asserts, "New Orleans been free now going on more than two decades—ever since the slave uprising in the first year of the war" (*BGD*). The enslaved peoples' emancipation does not mean that discriminatory practices in New Orleans have ceased, nor that reenslavement in this space is not a possibility. During the antebellum period, enslaved people and enslaved people who fled enslavement continuously feared being kidnapped, taken by those who enacted the Fugitive Slave Acts of 1793 and 1850. Enslaved people had constant anxiety that if they left their enslaver's property, they could be taken. It is no wonder that when reading slave narratives, many formerly enslaved people are portrayed as having PTSD. This fear is shown by Creeper as she ventures toward the Shá Roux, worrying that she may be caught.

The sexualization of the African American female adolescent is exposed in the incident at the Shá Roux. Bernstein discusses the Black-White dichotomy, using Stowe's Topsy and Eva to demonstrate (15). While publicized as significant to the abolitionist movement, as Bernstein demonstrates, Stowe's *Uncle Tom's Cabin* also works to include racial constructs, citing those about children as some of the most harmful. According to Bernstein, "Stowe configured Topsy and Eva as a polarized dyad, the 'two extremes of society': the 'fair' child with a 'golden head,' and the 'cringing' black child who had been viciously beaten by her previous owners" (15). Adding to her observations about characterization, Bernstein poses that Harriet Beecher Stowe combined the belief of the innocent child with minstrel character, thereby culminating in Topsy: "Topsy was an essentially innocent child who had been brutalized—hardened and 'wicked'— by slavery" (15). Clark gives readers Creeper, a child "hardened" by systemic racism, yet this is only an illusion. Creeper only presents herself as sophisticated regarding the ways of the world. In the characterization of Creeper, Clark takes possession of the antebellum typecasting of the Black child. While on the surface Creeper may present as independent, as without need for protection, this is a ruse to fool those she encounters. Upon entry to the brothel, a Scottish man mistakes Creeper for a boy, and then once he learns of her gender identity tries to prostitute the adolescent. When the man believes that Creeper is male, he looks out for Creeper, commenting on his young age. Once he discovers that Creeper is a girl—when she removes her hat—he preys on her, asking to purchase her. Clark's description of the moment is complex and must be examined from an intersectional angle: "'Not a lad,' I mutter, pulling off my cap to reveal a thick halo of black hair and a nut-brown face" (Clark). Creeper's gender identity is revealed at the same time as her racial identity, while her class is already known (she is an adolescent alone in a brothel, so assumptions about her parentage have been made by the male character).

It is Madame Diouf who acts as surrogate mother and protector to Creeper, saving her from the man, arranging for her to eat in the kitchen, and to take a bath and have her hair braided. She reminds "little creeping vice" that her birth name is that of Jacqueline, an act that both humanizes and feminizes the character. It is also Madame Diouf who, alongside the customers, objectifies these women, a group that formerly included Creeper's mother. Clark's novella, while placing women at the forefront of the plot—Creeper, Madame Diouf, the two Ursaline nuns, Féral, and the captain of the Midnight Robber, Ann-Marie—he also elects to still include stereotypes about African American women and women overall that objectify the body. In this reenvisioning of the past, Creeper's mother Rose has a sexual relationship with Captain Ann-Marie. While the character of Ann-Marie has promise—the captain is from the Free Caribbean, has a disability, and is a lesbian who oversees a multicultural male crew and her own airship—Creeper spends her formative years (which are glossed over) in a brothel. As an African American adolescent young woman, Clark has his Scottish male character make assumptions about Creeper based on the constructs that Bernstein has stated that Stowe reinforces in her novel. Once the Scottish john removes himself, Creeper is physically prodded by Madame Diouf, teased about her attire. Creeper hints to Madame Diouf that it is much more complicated than the simplistic just wanting to wear "boy's clothes";

it is a matter of protection. Madame Diouf asks, "Do you want to be mistaken for a boy?" a query to which Creeper responds, "On the streets, better people make that mistake" (*BGD*). Clark identifies all races within his novella as discriminating against one another, observing that there is fighting within the Black community.

Clark, a historian, identifies that free Black people were also enslavers and, in his novella, had them ensure that enslaved people were freed but only because they feared "an uprising." Further, when Madame Diouf mentions to Creeper that she could attend school if she wishes, the adolescent uses a slur to refer to herself: "pitènn's daughter" (*BGD*). Creeper repeats a Louisiana Creole word, one that is derogatory and gender-discriminatory toward Creeper and her parentage. Further, Madame Diouf becomes furious, citing that the slur, one enacted toward a child, has been made by formerly enslaved people. It appears that Clark is asserting that the characterization regarding African American young women does not come only from White enslavers, that the stereotypes have been taught to enslaved people as well. Clark portrays New Orleans as a space that, while some people embrace diversity and difference, it has been torn apart by enslavement. Through her journey toward maturation and self-acceptance, Creeper learns that she needs others in her life. Creeper accepts her culture: when asked about the importance of Oya in her life, Creeper reveals the god's position as surrogate mother, as guide, and as company. Creeper also accepts her identity; what Creeper disputes is needing others. Her team—those heroes that work to save the world—are also Othered: Sisters Agnès and Eunice, the biracial Ursaline nuns; Féral the White adolescent child of enslavers; and Ann-Marie, the captain of the airship. On the one hand, Clark offers readers a male view of a young woman's adolescence, and making her mother a sex worker is a questionable choice; on the other, it is a team of female heroes that joins with Creeper to save New Orleans while becoming Creeper's community. Ultimately, it is Creeper who is the hero, as she brings everyone together and exposes the Confederates for trying to enact the South's oppressive past. Ireland also chooses to include the child of a sex worker in her novel *Dread Nation*, but, in this case, Katherine is also biracial; the subject of passing is contemplated by some of Ireland's characters.

DREAD NATION AND *DEATHLESS DIVIDE*: UHURA, JANE, AND KATHERINE

In her analysis of films and television belonging to the speculative genre, Diana Adesola Mafe says, "Speculative fiction implies limitless potential where raced and gendered imaginaries are concerned" (3); however, she also observes the flaws in the genre with regard to the portrayal of Black female characters. Mafe begins her investigation of the speculative genre,[3] revolving her entire examination on the influential character of Lieutenant Uhura in *Star Trek*. Uhura's addition to television changed the face of the medium. Uhura (Nichelle Nichols) and Captain Kirk had the first interracial kiss on television, which William Shatner has stated had to happen as it felt right happening and both actors admitted taking great pains to ensure that the scene was not refilmed. Most importantly, Mafe finds that a Black woman is placed in an equal position as her White male counterparts when "her introductory shot situates her as a visual equal to her white male colleagues" (142). Uhura's character was so integral to supporting equity and presenting Black people positively for an international audience that when she wanted to step away from her role, Martin Luther King Jr. requested that she remain. Finally, Nichols was actively involved in recruiting people of color for NASA's space program in 1977 (Smithsonian). Although Mafe shows the integral part that Uhura played in media history, she also notes the rarity of Uhura's role. In reference to the films and television that Mafe selects for her study, she reveals that "where white and/or male protagonists are present, black female characters quickly become absent, reliant, or marginal" (8). In Ireland's *Dread Nation*, the writer casts White men and some White women in societal positions, oppressing and enslaving Black people. Janie, an African American female adolescent embodies CaShawn Thompson's #BlackGirlMagic, becoming a hero that subverts what Mafe sees as happening to Black women in film and television.

Ireland combines the epistolary format with the chapter format: at the start of most chapters Jane has written a letter to her mother, offering her a glossed-over sequence of events that are detailed within each chapter. By doing so, Ireland channels Shelley's format for *Frankenstein* while also rewriting the slave narrative. Rather than placing the letters around the narrative, thereby following the authenticating slave narrative structure, Ireland effectively heads chapters with a young girl's pleas for her mother. In following with the young adult novel structure, the initial novel must contain a plot where the adolescent splits with the parent's ideology, an act that enables the individuality of the adolescent. This structure, which is predominantly an approach for examining a White adolescent character, is problematic due to the societal positioning of the African American young woman. As it is with Creeper, information regarding Jane's birth and childhood is given in recollections of the past as Jane ensures that she retains a hold on the memories of her mother and her home. When *DN* opens, Jane is living at Miss Preston's School of Combat for Negro Girls in Baltimore, Maryland. Once African American young women reach adolescence, they are taken from their homes to a combat school (I will return to Ireland's explanation for this plot point later in the chapter). The brief childhood innocence for enslaved children of which Foster writes, for Jane it does not endure as she reveals that her mother attempted to drown her during her childhood. Throughout her journey Jane gives glimpses into a childhood spent on a plantation where she exists as the former enslavers' daughter but also as an African American child of a passing woman, a fact that is not revealed until near the close of the novel. Jane's seemingly idyllic childhood—she recollects playing with other children and being cared for by both her mother and Auntie Aggie—is punctuated by violent events, including her friend being killed by a shambler (zombie); her mother's strange treatment of her; and her murder of her father. These events work to save the life to which she had become accustomed, the only one she ever knew; once reality interjects into her memories, Jane's idealistic childhood fractures and she voices the trauma of her reality.

Audre Lorde states, "I write for those women who do not speak, for those who do not have a voice because they were so terrified, because we are taught to respect fear more than ourselves. We've been taught that silence would save us, but it won't" (Lorde). Jane writes letters to her mother along the lines of what Lorde has stated. To an adolescent young woman who has been made to leave the only home that she has known, Rose Hill Plantation, and her mother, who she believes has been protecting her from being taken away, Jane documents in letters her fears of not seeing her mother again. Although Jane does not receive a response from her mother—these letters are being withheld to lessen her hope for a future outside of attendant life—Jane continues to write. As Lorde writes for the voiceless, Jane as the novel begins is the hero in a way: she is the Angel of the Crossroads, venturing out of school at night to save people being attacked by shamblers. She rebels at the school, refusing to follow the rules, yet understands that she must be contrite, attempting to conform or she will be expelled from the school with no place to go. Jane is separated from her mother, but her circumstances differ from that of the slave narrative. Enslaved children were forcefully sold away from their families; it is intriguing that Ireland elects to have Jane choose to leave her home. As unfolds in the novel, Jane's mother is mentally disturbed, affected by the system of enslavement. It is for her mother more than for herself that Jane's writes. Her mother is not permitted as a biracial woman to identify as Black and to have a voice as a Black woman. Further, the manner in which Ireland crafts Momma makes the reader question if she prefers to identify as White rather than Black due to the lifestyle of privilege that comes along with being White in the South. While Jane portrays her mother as selfish—she has left Auntie Aggie to die along the trail to California—at the end of *Deathless Divide* (*DD*), Jane rejects her mother's life for herself and leaves her mother in Eden, Jane preferring her agency over the past, over the patriarchal enslavers life that has been taught to her mother. Jane recaptures her Angel of the Crossroads name in a way: "The old Jane would've gone along to get along, but that girl died in Nicodemus, and thank God" (Ireland, *DD* 540) while also somewhat rejecting her new persona as the Devil's Bride.

During her recollections in *DN*, Jane is placed on display during her mother's dinner parties as her mother seats her on her lap while she pets her and all the while Caucasian neighbors look on. Jane's mother treats her more as an accessory than a daughter; it is Auntie Aggie that encourages Jane to leave the plantation to attend school, thereby becoming an attendant. Once again, female characters take a place of prominence in this novel; however, the physicality of African American women is also at the forefront. The biracial women—Jane's mother and Katherine's mother—are sexualized. Jane's mother has a child with a dark complexion, so she is accused of having an affair with a formerly enslaved man. When she reflects on her life on the plantation, Jane is often confused, revering her mother yet only subconsciously aware that her mother's actions are abusive and conducted mainly from self-interest. After a letter in which Jane tries to discover if her mother has true affection for her (she crossed out the question), Jane deconstructs her mother' actions—she buys rebellious enslaved people—and the rumors that permeate their lives. Referencing societal construction and stereotypes about Black women, Mafe writes, "The black female body in speculative cinema risks even greater fetishization and exoticism because the genre . . . has been ubiquitously white and male on both authorship and audience" (7). American enslavement is built on the White, male vision of the American South. Using Jane, Ireland revises history, showing how the exoticization of Jane's mother affects her mental state. Reflecting on the rumor about her mother, Jane states, "But the strangest thing about Momma, the thing that made some of the neighbors smile tightly and alienated all the rest, is Momma's rumored penchant for field hands—the stronger, the darker, the better. They said she took them to bed like some kind of plantation Delilah, stealing their strength in order to keep herself young and healthy" (137). Jane identifies that the community, in order to oppress Momma's sexuality, attempts to place her in a container, controlling her as the spectacle. Jane's mother's behavior differs from what society expects of a White southern woman, so she is labeled as a promiscuous woman and a magical being, thereby removing her humanity.

Boster analyzes the treatment of enslaved people, focusing on physical disabilities and mental illness. Inspecting the commodification of enslaved people, Boster observes, "Presale inspections . . . provided slaves themselves with an opportunity to participate in assessments of their soundness and value, entering into a dialogue with traders and buyers using the same language of the market" (86–87). Further examining the interaction, Boster identifies that this contact between enslaved people and enslavers either guaranteed purchase or rejection (87). The enslaved people were then involved in their commodification, a condition that would have elicited feelings of guilt even though enslavement was not a choice. Although Jane blames her mother for her actions, she does not take into account that her mother feels guilt for being born Black. In *Deathless Divide*, when Jane tries to speak to her mother about the past, Momma flatly refuses to revisit, preferring avoidance over confronting her attempted murder of her child. Sethe kills her child so to save her from enslavement; Momma's mental illness causes her to reject her child because she is born with a dark complexion, an illness brought on by the influence of enslavement in the American South. Throughout both novels, Jane appears obsessed with Katherine's light complexion and repeatedly encourages her to reject her identity as a Black woman, passing for White instead.

In his examination of the Harlem Renaissance, Steven Watson explains that writers such as Wallace Thurman were concerned about acceptance in the community because of the existence of colorism. Watson offers, "The fine calibration of degrees on the melanin scale can be seen in novels, where fictional characters are identified by their precise shade, in the fascination with 'passing' for white, and in the rich vocabulary—both formal and slang—developed to describe skin color" (86–87). Further, one of the most important literary contributions from the Harlem Renaissance and in American literature overall is Nella Larsen's *Passing*, a narrative in which Larsen deftly reveals the circumstances, namely systemic racism and feelings of inferiority, that lead to the rejection of a character's identity as Black. Larsen is not the only author that has discussed the color line, colorism, and passing. Kimberly Snyder Manganelli analyzes the rise of the Tragic Mulatta character; for this examination, her work with this character and New Orleans is compelling. Jane's friend from Miss Preston's, Katherine, grows up in a New Orleans brothel as her mother is a sex worker; this environment may appear to be the reason why Katherine ended up at the school, but as it is with Jane, it is her racial identity and societal discriminatory practices that force her away from home. Manganelli explains that in New Orleans in the nineteenth century, biracial and/or multiracial people were not welcome in New Orleans due to the belief that they could be identified as White rather than Black (37–38). Further, biracial and/or multiracial women were involved in "plaçage, an institution that allowed free women of color to arrange unions with affluent white men" (38). While Jane is the protagonist, the addition of Katherine's story to the second novel and her voice as a narrator make a more balanced plot.

Katherine and Jane are alternating narrators in *Deathless Divide*, Ireland juxtaposing the friends' accounts of reaching California and finding one another again. Katherine is a more developed character: she is aware of her sexuality and of how people treat her due to her complexion and her beauty. When the initial town falls due to Gideon's experimentation and the group is on its way to Nicodemus, the friends talk, Jane drawing information from Katherine about her past. To Jane, Katherine discloses that her mother is a plaçee and that she runs a brothel. She reflects on her childhood, identifying to herself that "There were happy moments, but mostly I remember the fear of my body changing and growing, because I knew at some point I would have to take a husband, or a patron, like my mother and her friends did. That was just the way of things back in New Orleans" (Ireland, *DD* 360). At the training school, Katherine conceals her mother's societal position, afraid of what other would think of her. Once forced to leave, and she becomes more trustful of Jane, Katherine tells her more about what life is like for a biracial woman in New Orleans. As with Jane, who is comfortable identifying as pansexual (she has a relationship with Callie and Jackson), Katherine accepts her sexuality. Katherine reflects, "The thought of a man's hands on my body left me cold, and it still does. Nor is the idea of a female companion, like Miss Mellie May's lost love, something I desire. But until I ran away, there was never any kind of a hope for any other kind of a life" (*DD* 361). It is in *Deathless Divide* that Katherine reveals she flees New Orleans at thirteen, hiding in the bayous and subsequently training with the Laveaus, the most powerful women in New Orleans. Manganelli's definition of the Tragic Mulatta brings to mind Katherine's characterization: "Represented as being both white and black, chaste and wanton, free and enslaved, the Tragic Mulatta's mixed-race blood was believed to imbue her with the fair skin and refined manners of her white sisters, but beneath the surface lingered a trace of Africa that supposedly incited passion and sexual wantonness" (39). Throughout the series, Katherine is repeatedly approached by men for either a sexual relationship or, if it is believed that she is White, marriage. Katherine is uncomfortable with this unwanted attention but understands from what she has learned from New Orleans' free women of color that flirting ensures that she gets what she needs. Jane tries to force Katherine to pass for White, not comprehending why she refuses and becomes upset at the idea. Katherine is secure in her identity: she is a Black woman who is currently not interested in a sexual relationship. Unlike Jane, who is unsure of herself, Katherine is self-aware, her maturation revolving around trust and friendships. It is society that has categorized Katherine as the Tragic Mulatta, not Katherine herself.

CONCLUSION: THE HEROES AND THE NOVEL'S INCLUSIVITY

Jane's physicality is revealed in the opening of *DN* as she learns how to use a scythe during Miss Duncan's combat class. Regarding the slave narrative, it is common for an enslaved woman to be portrayed as only a physical being, as one who is overly strong and capable of great physical feats—in other words, to be shown as a stereotype. It is challenging for the reader that Ireland has created a character that is intelligent and heroic—Jane repeatedly saves her friends and herself from certain death—she is also mean to her friends and is shown as superhuman when battling large groups of shamblers. Ultimately, Jane is successful in the initial novel; she and her friends survive their ordeal, venturing forth to search for her mother in California and, in the second novel, for Gideon after he experiments on the people of Nicodemus, who are primarily Black. Jane blends her personas Angel of the Crossroads and the Devil's Bride as she symbolically walks away from Eden and her old life with her mother as *Deathless Divide* concludes.

Mafe poignantly offers that "The Western tradition of white men studying black women in the name of so-called science cannot be disassociate form the Western tradition of white men imagining black women in the name of science fiction" (7). Ireland rewrites history from a Black woman's point of view, having Jane and Katherine not only learn how to trust one another thereby becoming a community but also joining forces to bring Gideon to justice for his experimentation on African Americans. On the one hand, as writer, Ireland calls attention to Tuskegee and Henrietta Lacks via her young female heroes. On the other hand, Jane and Katherine symbolically ride off into the sunset at the end of the second novel because their #BlackGirlMagic makes them different in American society: they refuse to assimilate so they must spend their lives on the margins of society.

On a final note, Ireland's portrayal of people of various racial identities is disconcerting, especially for an adolescent readership. While the alternative historical structure of the novels is understood, it is upsetting that stereotypes about Asian immigrants and Native Americans especially have been included within the novel. Further, at the close of *DN* Ireland adds a note that her combat schools are based on Indian Affairs schools, a questionable choice. This is a traumatic period in American and Canadian history for Indigenous people, when they were forcefully taken from their homes by Caucasian people (government officials and Catholic Church representatives), forced to reject their identities as Indigenous people.[4]

The question always remains: what responsibility do writers have to adolescent readers? Is it enough to try to reclaim the past through repetition, or in young adult speculative literature should the writer not repeat past stereotypes, instead signaling inclusivity for adolescent readers?

NOTES

INTRODUCTION

1. The comic book character Black Panther initially appeared 1 Jul. 1966 in the Fantastic Four comic.
2. The report examines statistical data regarding the racial and gender identities of actors in films and television. In the 2020 UCLA report, Black actors have 15.7 percent roles; this is an increase from 2018 (14.9 percent) and 2017 (9.0 percent).
3. The largest increase for Black women in film happened from 2017 (29/1281) to 2018 (62/1089).
4. It has taken from 2011 (25.6 percent) to 2020 (47.8 percent) for there to be an increase in female casting (*Hollywood Diversity Report 2021*: "Lead Actor Gender, Theatrical/Streaming Films, 2011–2020," chart 14).
5. Katheryn Bigelow won for *The Hurt Locker* (2009), Chloe Zhao for *Nomadland* (2021), and Jane Campion for *The Power of the Dog* (2022).
6. Regina King was nominated for Best Director at the Golden Globes for *One Night in Miami* (2021).
7. Wonder Woman grossed over $800 million worldwide (https://www.imdb.com/title/tt0451279/).
8. Margaret Walker's proto-neo-slave narrative, *Jubilee* (1966), also received what may be considered "mainstream" academic attention. Until the twenty-first century, academia was canonized in accordance with T. S. Eliot's canon. While working on my BA with Honours in English in Canada, the "joke" was that literature students only study "dead, White, European guys." The aforementioned may explain why African American women's literature was not awarded the attention that it deserved until Morrison.
9. Lewis's website refers to the film as Afropunk. The film was nominated for numerous Canadian and American cinematic awards (winning in costume and special mention), again reiterating interest in this field. Media coming from a Canadian market are notorious for having problems obtaining popularity in an American market.
10. For clarification, this book focuses on the American slave narrative.

11. For further reading, see Stephen Crawford's contribution to a chapter, "The Slave Family: A View from the Slave Narratives," in *Strategic Factors in Nineteenth Century American Economic History: A Volume to Honor Robert W. Fogel*, ed. Claudia Goldin and Hugh Rockoff (U Chicago P, 1992), pp. 331–50.

12. Term: women who are over the age of sixty-five. This is the least agist term I know of to use when referring to women sixty-five+.

13. Goyal applies the neo-slave narrative to people without connection to the American antebellum period or to the Atlantic slave trade in general. While there have been varied forms of enslavement historically worldwide, the neo-slave narrative is a literary form with connection to Black people and the aforementioned periods of enslavement.

14. See also Colson Whitehead's *Underground Railroad* (2016) as an example of the twenty-first-century neo-slave narrative and magical realism.

15. Britain is well known for disputing that it had enslavement on its soil (that it was relegated only to the colonies); however, slave narratives have shown that enslaved people who went to England remained enslaved in England.

16. The *1619 Project* posits that American enslavement is an integral part of American history, which some historians studying American history have been arguing for some time. There has been some controversy associated with the interdisciplinary project's preface, however, due to Nikole Hannah-Jones's claims regarding the Revolutionary War and reasons for independence, specifically citing the preservation of American enslavement.

17. *Legendborn* is the initial novel in the Legendborn Cycle, the second of which, *Bloodmarked*, was published in 2022.

18. The publishing industry has been problematic, much like Hollywood, in that publications in varied genres have been released that readers have found discriminatory. Further, literature may be optioned on the basis of what publishers believe readers want instead of what they actually want.

19. During the summer of 2020, many YA writers took to Twitter to express the inequalities in the publishing industry.

20. The National Humanities Center resource, "Slave Auctions: Selections from 19th-century Narratives for Formerly Enslaved African Americans," identifies that between 1765–1865, 102 slave narratives in varied forms were released. The publications' expectations were made clear by the fact that many came from abolitionist societies.

CHAPTER 1: SHERRI L. SMITH'S *ORLEANS* AND KAREN SANDLER'S *TANKBORN*: THE FEMALE LEADER, THE NEO-SLAVE, AND TWENTY-FIRST-CENTURY YOUNG ADULT AFROFUTURISM

1. As with Okorafor's Phoenix, the treatment of Fen alludes to that of Henrietta Lacks at Johns Hopkins Hospital and the men in the Tuskegee syphilis trials.

2. Unless used to refer to an Indigenous cultural celebration, the terminology is problematic and should not be used.

CHAPTER 2: THE SAFETY OF SPACE IN NNEDI OKORAFOR'S *THE BOOK OF PHOENIX* AND *BINTI*

1. The study to which I refer was published in 2009 and primarily dealt with British young adult science fiction.

2. When applying theory that analyzes a particular racial group (in this case, the text in question primarily concentrates on Caucasian and British), the reader must be cognizant that not all aspects will work, that the theory may only be significant for that racial and national group.

CHAPTER 3: AFROHORROR AND THE GENDERED NARRATOR: PROGRESSION AND REGRESSION OF THE ADOLESCENT FEMALE ACTIVIST CHARACTER IN THE DEVIL'S WAKE SERIES AND THE PARABLES SERIES

1. The butch and femme lesbian identity constructs are common and accepted in the LGBTQ2S community. The manner in which Ancrum forms these two identities in her novel is problematic, offering negative images of gay women.

2. It is implied that Ryann is White; she is described as having red hair and living in a trailer. In fact, no race is offered for this character, or her family, when race has been stated for the remainder of her friend circle in the novel. Startling, Ancrum has made Ryann the "White trailer park trash" stereotype, seemingly in an effort to reclaim the image.

3. This is a portion of the original, famous quotation. The original contains the n-word and does not need to be repeated here.

4. Du Bois was a misogynist and a classist.

CHAPTER 4: THE BIRACIAL FEMALE PROTAGONIST, TRAUMA, AND MEMORY IN A. J. HARTLEY'S *STEEPLEJACK*

1. Due to Rowling's support of a Black actor, the writer has been referenced here. Rowling's transwomen exclusionary practices are acknowledged as unacceptable.

2. Hartley teaches performance at UNC at Charlotte, holding the position of Robinson Professor of Shakespeare Studies.

3. Ulanowicz's book cited here won the Children's Literature Association Book Award in 2015.

4. It has been announced that the *1619 Project* (the *New York Times* research project helmed by journalist Hannah-Jones) will be brought to Hulu via docuseries. This project places American history in context, pinpointing the date of the initial enslaved people's arrival in America as integral to America's evolution.

5. Bailey and Sawyer are referring to Tolkien-type fantasies in particular.

CHAPTER 5: SELF-IMAGE AND NARRATION IN THE YOUNG ADULT STEAMPUNK NOVELS *THE BLACK GOD'S DRUMS* AND THE DREAD NATION SERIES

1. A West African god.

2. See Carby's groundbreaking work, *Reconstructing Womanhood: The Emergence of the Afro-American Woman Novelist*. Carby poses that White southern womanhood is a construct in itself, that it directly impacts the construct(s) regarding Black womanhood. This note posits that the "innocence" of White enslavers regarding sex and rape is constructed, that female enslavers were aware of the physical violations of the enslaved women's bodies.

3. Mafe identifies that she sees science fiction as a subgenre of speculative fiction (3). I disagree, classifying science fiction and speculative fiction as separate genres.

4. Starting in 2020, the remains of Indigenous children have been found on the sites of residential schools, with connections to the Canadian government and the Catholic Church. Investigations are under way. In 2021, it was announced that sites in the United States will also be searched for children's remains. The report was released in May 2022; for further information, see https://www.npr.org/2022/05/11/1098276649/u-s-report-details-burial-sites-linked-to-boarding-schools-for-native-americans.

WORKS CITED

Ancrum, K[ayla]. *The Weight of the Stars*. Imprint, 2019.
Archer, Jermaine O. *Antebellum Slave Narratives: Cultural and Political Expressions of Africa*. Routledge, 2013.
Baccolini, Raffiella, and Tom Moylan. "Introduction: Dystopia and Histories." *Dark Horizons: Science Fiction and the Dystopian Imagination*, edited by Raffiella Baccolini and Tom Moyan, Routledge, 2003. Kindle.
Bailey, K. V., and Andy Sawyer. "The Janus Perspective: Science Fiction and the Young Adult Reader in Britain." *Young Adult Science Fiction*, edited by C. W. Sullivan, Greenwood Press, 1999, pp. 55–71.
Barnes, Brooks. "Disney Finds a Cure for the Common Stereotype With 'Doc McStuffins.'" *New York Times*, 30 Jul. 2012, https://www.nytimes.com/2012/07/31/arts/television/disneys-doc-mcstuffins-connects-with-black-viewers.html. Accessed 30 Jul. 2012.
Barnes, Steven, and Tananarive Due. *Devil's Wake*. Atria, 2012. Kindle.
Barnes, Steven, and Tananarive Due. *Domino Falls*. Atria, 2013. Kindle.
Barr, Marlene S. "The Laugh of Anansi: Why SF Is Pertinent to Black Children's Literature Pedagogy." *Black and Brown Planets*, edited by Isiah Lavender III, UP of Mississippi, 2014, pp. 83–97.
Basu, Balaka, Katherine R. Broad, and Carrie Hintz. "Introduction." *Dystopian Fiction for Young Adults: Brave New Teenagers*, edited by Balaka Basu, Katherine R. Broad, and Carrie Hintz, Routledge, 2014, pp. 1–15.
Beaulieu, Elizabeth Ann. *Black Women Writers and the American Neo-Slave Narrative: Femininity Unfettered*. Greenwood Press, 1999.
Bernstein, Robin. *Racial Innocence: Performing American Childhood from Slavery to Civil Rights*. New York UP, 2011.
Boster, Dea H. *African American Slavery and Disability: Bodies, Property, and Power in the Antebellum South, 1800–1860*. 2013. Routledge, 2014.
Bradford, Clare. "Race, Ethnicity and Colonialism." *The Routledge Companion to Children's Literature*, edited by David Rudd, Routledge, 2010, pp. 39–50.
"Brown Girl Begins." SharonLewis. 2022, https://www.thesharonlewis.com/work/brown-girl-begins/. Accessed 15 Mar. 2022

Bruce, Dickson D., Jr. "Politics in the Slave Narrative." *The Cambridge Companion to the African American Slave Narrative*, edited by Audrey Fisch, Cambridge UP, 2007, pp. 28–43.

Budick, Emily Miller. "Absence, Loss, and the Space of History in Toni Morrison's *Beloved*." *Arizona Quarterly*, vol. 48, no. 2, 1992, pp. 117–38. Project Muse. https://doi.org/10.1353/arq.1992.0008. Accessed 11 Apr. 2018.

Butler, Octavia E. "A Conversation with Octavia E. Butler." In *Conversations with Octavia Butler*, edited by Consuela Francis, UP of Mississippi, 2010, pp. 206–12.

Butler, Octavia E. *Parable of the Sower*. 1993. Open Road Media, 2019. Kindle.

Butler, Octavia E. *Parable of the Talents*. 1998. Open Road Media, 2012. Kindle.

Carby, Hazel. *Reconstructing Womanhood: The Emergence of the Afro-American Woman Novelist*. Oxford UP, 1987.

Clark, P. Djèlí. *The Black God's Drums*. Doherty, 2018. Kindle.

Connolly, Paula T. *Slavery in American Children's Literature, 1790–2010*. U Iowa P, 2013.

Couzelis, Mary J. "The Future is Pale: Race in Contemporary Young Adult Dystopian Novels." In *Dystopian Fiction for Young Adults: Brave New Teenagers*, edited by Balaka Basu, Katherine R. Broad, and Carrie Hintz, Routledge, 2014, pp. 131–44.

Crenshaw, Kimberlé. "Black Girls Matter." *MS*. 23 Jun. 2015, https://msmagazine.com/2015/06/23/black-girls-matter/. Accessed 10 Feb. 2021.

Day, Sara, Miranda Green-Barteet, and Amy Montz. "Introduction: From 'New Woman' to 'Future Girl': The Roots and the Rise of the Female Protagonist in Contemporary Young Adult Dystopias." In *Female Rebellion in Young Adult Dystopian Fiction*, edited by Sara Day, Miranda Green-Barteet, and Amy Montz, Ashgate, 2014, pp. 1–14.

Deonn, Tracy. *Legendborn*. McElderry, 2020. Kindle.

Dery, Mark. "Black to the Future: Interviews with Samuel R. Delany, Greg Tate, and Tricia Rose." In *Flame Wars: The Discourse of Cyberculture*. Duke UP, 1994, pp. 179–222.

Dixon, Melvin. "Singing Swords: The Literary Legacy of Slavery." In *The Slave's Narratives*, edited by Charles T. Davis and Henry Louis Gates, Jr., Oxford UP, 1985, pp. 298–317.

Doll, Jen. "The Ongoing Problem of Race in YA." *The Atlantic*, 26 April 2012, https://www.theatlantic.com/entertainment/archive/2012/04/ongoing-problem-race-y/328841/. Accessed Jun. 2017.

Douglass, Frederick. *Narrative of the Life of Frederick Douglass, an American Slave. Narrative of the Life of Frederick Douglass, an American Slave & Incidents in the Life of a Slave Girl, Written by Herself*. Modern Library, 2004. Kindle.

Driscoll, Catherine. *Teen Film: A Critical Introduction*. Berg, 2011.
Dubey, Madhu. "'Even Some Fiction Might Be Useful': African American Women Novelists." In *The Cambridge Companion to African American Women's Literature*, edited by Angelyn Mitchell and Danille K. Taylor, Cambridge UP, 2009, pp. 150–67.
Durgan, Jessica. "Uptops and Sooties: Neo-Victorian Representations of Race and Class in Gail Carriger's *Finishing School* Books." In *The Victorian Era in Twenty-First Century Children's and Adolescent Literature and Culture*, edited by Sonya Sawyer Fritz and Sara K. Day, Routledge, 2018, pp. 214–33.
Elphick, Keith. "Discursive Transgressions and Ideological Negotiations: From Orwell's *1984* to Butler's *Parable of the Sower*." In *Environments in Science Fiction: Essays on Alternative Spaces*, edited by Susan M. Bernardo, McFarland, 2014, pp. 171–90.
Equiano, Olaudah. *The Interesting Narrative of the Life of Olaudah Equiano, or Gustavus Vassa, the African. Written by Himself*. In *The Classic Slave Narratives*. 1987. Signet, 2002, pp. 15–247.
Eyerman, Ron. *Cultural Trauma: Slavery and the Formation of African American Identity*. Cambridge UP, 2001.
Flagel, Nadine. "'It's Almost Like Being There': Speculative Fiction, Slave Narrative, and the Crisis of Representation in Octavia Butler's *Kindred*." *Canadian Review of American Studies*, vol. 42, no. 2, 2012, pp. 216–45.
Foster, Frances Smith. *Witnessing Slavery: The Development of Ante-bellum Slave Narratives*. 2nd ed., U of Wisconsin P, 1979.
Fulton, DoVeanna S. *Speaking Power: Black Feminist Orality in Women's Narratives*. State U of New York P, 2006.
Gates, Henry Louis, Jr. "Introduction." In *The Classic Slave Narratives*. 1987. Signet, 2002, pp. 1–14.
Gibbs, Alan. *Contemporary American Trauma Narratives*. Edinburgh UP, 2014.
Gilbert-Hickey, Meghan. "'Good and Safe': Violence and the Gothic Pedagogy of Appropriateness in the Hunger Games Trilogy." *Storytelling: A Critical Journal of Popular Narrative*, 2014, pp. 7–18, https://www.academia.edu/12813693/_Good_and_Safe_Race_Violence_and_the_Gothic_Pedagogy_of_Appropriateness_in_The_Hunger_Games_Trilogy_. Accessed 1 Mar. 2015.
Glasner, Eli. "'We Are ready, We've Been ready': Black Panther Ushers in a New Wave of Black Sci-Fi." *CBCnews*, 10 Feb. 2018, http://www.cbc.ca/news/entertainment/black-panther-sci-fi-diversity-1.4528305. Accessed 10 Feb. 2018.
Gomez, Jewelle. "Foreword." In *The Gilda Stories*. City Lights Publishers, 1991. Kindle.
Goyal, Yogita. *Runaway Genres: The Global Afterlives of Slavery*. New York UP, 2019.
Harris, Trudier. *Saints, Sinners, Saviors: Strong Black Women in African American Literature*. Palgrave, 2001.

Harris-Perry, Melissa V. *Sister Citizen: Shame, Stereotypes, and Black Women in America*. Yale UP, 2011.

Hartley, A. J. "Chains," edited by Diana Pho. Tor, 2016, https://www.tor.com/2016/06/22/chains/. Accessed 28 Apr. 2017.

Hartley, A. J *Firebrand*. Tor, 2017. Kindle.

Hartley, A. J. *The Guardian*. Tor, 2018. Kindle.

Hartley, A. J. "A Head for Heights: The History Behind Steeplejack." *Tor.com*, 28 Apr. 2017, http://www.tor.com/2017/04/28/a-head-for-heights-the-history-behind-steeplejack/.

Hartley, A. J. *Steeplejack*. Tor, 2016. Kindle.

Hartley, A. J. "Writing POC While White." Tor/Forge Blog, 6 Jun. 2016, https://www.torforgeblog.com/2016/06/06/writing-poc-while-white/. Accessed 25 Mar. 2021.

Hill Collins, Patricia. *Black Sexual Politics: African Americans, Gender, and the New Racism*. Routledge, 2005.

hooks, bell. *Ain't I a Woman: Black Women and Feminism*. South End Press, 1981.

hooks, bell. *Belonging: A Culture of Place*. Routledge, 2009.

Hunt, Darnell, and Ana-Christina Ramón. "Part 1: Film." *Hollywood Diversity Report 2021: Pandemic in Progress*. UCLA: College of Social Sciences, 2021, https://socialsciences.ucla.edu/wp-content/uploads/2021/04/UCLA-Hollywood-Diversity-Report-2021-Film-4-22-2021. Accessed 1 Mar. 2022.

Hutcheon, Linda with Siobhan O'Flynn. *A Theory of Adaptation*. 2006. 2nd ed. Routledge, 2013.

Ireland, Justina. *Deathless Divide*. Balzer + Bray, 2020.

Ireland, Justina. *Dread Nation*. Balzer + Bray, 2018.

Jacobs, Harriet [Brent, Linda]. *Incidents in the Life of a Slave Girl, Written by Herself. Narrative of the Life of Frederick Douglass, an American Slave & Incidents in the Life of a Slave Girl, Written by Herself*. 1861. Modern Library, 2004. Kindle.

Kawin, Bruce. *Horror and the Horror Film*. Anthem Press, 2012.

Keckley, Elizabeth. *Behind the Scenes. By Elizabeth Keckley, Formerly a Slave, but More Recently Modiste, and Friend to Mrs. Abraham Lincoln. Or, Thirty Years a Slave, and Four Years in the White House*. 1868. Modern Library, n.d. Kindle.

Kilgore, De Witt Douglas. "Afrofuturism." In *Oxford Handbook to Science Fiction*, edited by Rob Latham, Oxford UP, 2014, pp. 561–72.

King, Debra Walker. *African Americans and the Culture of Pain*. U of Virginia P, 2008.

King, Debra Walker. "Writing in Red Ink." In *Body Politics and the Fictional Double*, edited by Debra Walker King, Indiana UP, 2000, pp. 56–70.

Koss, Melanie D. "Young Adult Novels with Multiple Narrative Perspectives: The Changing Nature of YA Literature." *Alan Review*, vol. 36, no. 3, 2009, https://doi.org/10.21061/alan.v36i3.a.9. Accessed 15 Mar. 2015.

Kritzer, Naomi. *Catfishing on CatNet*. TorTeen, 2019.
Lavender, Isiah. *Race in Science Fiction*. Indiana UP, 2011.
Lemon, Don. *This Is the Fire: What I Say to My Friends about Racism*. Little, Brown and Company, 2021.
Leonard, Elizabeth Anne. "Race and Ethnicity in Science Fiction." In *The Cambridge Companion to Science Fiction*, edited by Edward James and Farah Mendlesohn, Cambridge UP, 2003, pp. 253–63.
Levitas, Ruth. *The Concept of Utopia*. Peter Lang, 2010.
Lorde, Audre. "15 Inspiring Audre Lorde Quotes to Help You Find Your Voice." *Entity Magazine*. 28 Sep. 2017, https://www.entitymag.com/audre-lorde-quotes-voice/. Accessed 11 Jul. 2022.
Lundquist, Lynne, and Gary Westfahl. "Coming of Age in Fantasyland: The Self-Parenting Child in Walt Disney Animated Films." In *Nursery Realms: Children in the Worlds of Science Fiction, Fantasy, and Horror*, edited by Gary Westfahl and George Slusser, U Georgia P, 1999, pp. 161–70.
MacCann, Donnarae. *White Supremacy in Children's Literature: Characterizations of African Americans, 1830–1900*. Routledge, 1998.
Mafe, Diana Adesola. *Where No Black Woman Has Gone Before: Subversive Portrayals in Speculative Film and TV*. U Texas P, 2018.
Manganelli, Kimberly Snyder. *Transatlantic Spectacles of Race: The Tragic Mulatta and the Tragic Muse*. Rutgers UP, 2012.
Mann, Catherine. "*The Book of Phoenix*. Book Review." Rev. of *The Book of Phoenix*. The British Fantasy Society, 2015, http://www.britishfantasysociety.org/reviews/the-book-of-phoenix-book-review/. Accessed 15 Jan. 2017.
Marotta, Melanie A. "Liberation through Acceptance of Nature and Technology in Octavia E. Butler's 'Parable of the Sower.'" *Theory in Action*, vol. 3, no. 1, 2010, pp. 38–51.
McArthur, Sherell A. "Black Girls and Critical Media Literacy for Social Activism." *English Education*, vol. 48, no. 4, 2016, pp. 362–79. https://www.jstor.org/stable/26492574. Accessed 28 Feb. 2021.
McConnell, Kelsey. "These Are All the Octavia Butler Adaptations Currently in Development." *The Portalist*, 24 Dec. 2020, https://theportalist.com/octavia-butler-adaptations-in-development. Accessed 13 Dec. 2021.
McDuffe, Kristi. "Technology and Models of Literacy in Young Adult Dystopian Fiction." In *Dystopian Fiction for Young Adults: Brave New Teenagers*, edited by Balaka Basu, Katherine R. Broad, and Carrie Hintz, Routledge, 2014, pp. 145–56.
Meeusen, Meghann. *Children's Books on the Big Screen*. UP of Mississippi, 2020.
Mendlesohn, Farah. *The Inter-Galactic Playground: A Critical Study of Children's and Teens' Science Fiction*. McFarland, 2009.
Morrison, Toni. *Beloved*. Vintage, 2007.

Moylan, Tom. *Scraps of the Untainted Sky: Science Fiction, Utopia, Dystopia.* Routledge, 2000.

National Humanities Center. "Slave Auctions: Selections from 19th-century Narratives for Formerly Enslaved African Americans." In *National Humanities Center Resource Toolbox: The Making of African American Identity: Vol. I, 1500–1865,* http://nationalhumanitiescenter.org/pds/maai/enslavement/text2/slaveauctions. Accessed 1 Mar. 2022.

Newman, Judie. "Slave Narratives and Neo-Slave Narratives." In *The Cambridge Companion to the Literature of the American South.* Cambridge UP, 2013, pp. 26–38.

Okorafor, Nnedi. *Binti.* Doherty, 2015. Kindle.

Okorafor, Nnedi. *Binti: Home.* Doherty, 2017. Kindle.

Okorafor, Nnedi. *The Book of Phoenix.* DAW Books, 2015. Kindle.

Okorafor, Nnedi. "Hello, Moto." Tor.com, 2011, https://www.tor.com/2011/11/02/hello-moto/. Accessed 30 Jun. 2017.

Olney, James. "'I Was Born': Slave Narratives, Their Status as Autobiography and as Literature." In *The Slave's Narrative,* edited by Charles T. Davis and Henry Louis Gates, Jr. Oxford University Press, 1985, pp. 148–75.

Porter, Rick. "FX Nabs Octavia E. Butler's Kindred." *Hollywood Reporter,* 8 Mar. 2021, https://www.hollywoodreporter.com/tv/tv-news/fx-adapting-octavia-e-butlers-kindred-4145371/. Accessed 8 Mar. 2021.

Prince, Mary. *The History of Mary Prince, A West Indian Slave. Related by Herself.* In *The Classic Slave Narratives.* 1987. Signet, 2002, pp. 249–316.

Pulliam, June. "Real or Not Real—Katniss Everdeen Loves Peeta Melark: The Lingering Effects of Discipline in the Hunger Games Trilogy." *Female Rebellion in Young Adult Dystopian Fiction,* edited by Sara Day, Miranda Green-Barteet, and Amy Montz, Ashgate, 2014, pp. 171–85.

Ratcliffe, Rebecca. "JK Rowling Tells of Anger at Attacks on Casting of Back Hermione." *Guardian,* 5 Jun. 2016, https://www.theguardian.com/stage/2016/jun/05/harry-potter-jk-rowling-black-hermione. Accessed 30 Jun. 2017.

@rosierambles. "There is no topic. . . ." *Twitter,* 23 Nov. 2020, 1:27 p.m.

Rowe, Karen E. "Feminism and Fairy Tales." In *Folk & Fairy Tales,* edited by Martin Hallett and Barbara Karasek. 2nd ed., Broadview Press, 1996, pp. 325–45.

Rushdy, Ashraf. *Neo-Slave Narratives.* Oxford UP, 1999.

Rushdy, Ashraf H. A. *Remembering Generations: Race and Family in Contemporary African American Fiction.* University of North Carolina Press, 2003.

Sandler, Karen. *Tankborn.* TU, 2011. Kindle.

Santamaria, Xiomara. "Black Womenhood in North American Women's Slave Narratives." In *The Cambridge Companion to the African American Slave Narrative,* edited by Audrey Fisch, Cambridge UP, 2007, pp. 232–45.

Sargent, Lyman Tower. "The Three Faces of Utopianism Revisited." *Utopian Studies*, vol. 5, no. 1, 1994, pp. 1–37, https://www.jstor.org/stable/20719246. Accessed 28 Feb. 2018.

Sargent, Lyman Tower. *Utopianism: A Very Short Introduction*. Oxford UP, 2010. Kindle.

Scott, Lynn Orilla. "Autobiography: Slave Narratives." In *Oxford Research Encyclopedia of Literature*. Oxford UP, 26 Jul. 2017, https://doi.org/10.1093/acrefore/9780190201098.013.658. Accessed 19 Mar. 2021.

Sims, David. "A Young Adult Trend Fizzles with *The Death Cure*." *Atlantic*, 25 Jan. 2018, https://www.theatlantic.com/entertainment/archive/2018/01/the-maze-runner-death-cure-review/551459/. Accessed 25 Jan. 2018.

Sinanan, Kerry. "The Slave Narrative and the Literature of Abolition." In *The Cambridge Companion to the African American Slave Narrative*. Cambridge UP, 2007, pp. 61–80.

Smith, Katharine Capshaw. *Children's Literature of the Harlem Renaissance*. Indiana UP, 2004.

Smith, Sherri L. *Orleans*. Penguin, 2013. Kindle.

Smith, Valerie. "Neo-Slave Narratives." *The Cambridge Companion to the African American Slave Narrative*, edited by Audrey Fisch, Cambridge UP, pp. 168–88.

Smithsonian National Air and Space Museum. "Margaret Weitekamp, curator and department chair." Facebook Live, 7 Feb. 2018, https://www.facebook.com/9739297796/videos/10155083479052797. Accessed 30 Mar. 2021.

Stepto, Robert B. *From behind the Veil: A Study of Afro-American Narrative*. 2nd ed. University of Illinois Press, 1991.

Stewart, Ian. "Number Symbolism." In *Encyclopedia Britannica*, https://www.britannica.com/topic/number-symbolism#ref248162. Accessed 1 Feb. 2018.

Sullivan, C. W. "American Young Adult Science Fiction since 1947." In *Young Adult Science Fiction*, edited by C. W. Sullivan, Praeger, 1993, pp. 21–35.

Thomson, Rosemarie Garland. *Extraordinary Bodies: Figuring Physical Disability in American Culture and Literature*. Columbia UP, 1997.

Trites, Roberta Seelinger. *Disturbing the Universe: Power and Repression in Adolescent Literature*. U Iowa P, 2004.

Trites, Roberta Seelinger. *Waking Sleeping Beauty: Feminist Voices in Children's Novels*. U Iowa P, 1997.

Ulanowicz, Anastasia. *Second-Generation Memory and Contemporary Children's Literature: Ghost Images*. 2013. Routledge, 2018.

Varsam, Maria. "Concrete Dystopia: Slavery and Its Others." *Dark Horizons: Science Fiction and the Dystopian Imagination*, edited by Raffiella Baccolini and Tom Maylan, Routledge, 2003. Kindle.

Waldman, Katy. "Slave or Enslaved Person?" *Slate*, 19 May 2015, https://slate.com/human-interest/2015/05/historians-debate-whether-to-use-the-term-slave-or-enslaved-person.html. Accessed 9 Mar. 2021.

Watson, Steven. *The Harlem Renaissance: Hub of African-American Culture, 1920–1930*. Pantheon, 1995.

Williams, Imogen Russell. "Where Are the YA Books? And Who Is Reading Them?" *Guardian*, 31 Jul. 2014, https://www.theguardian.com/books/booksblog/2014/jul/31/ya-books-reads-young-adult-teen-new-adult-books. Accessed 1 Oct. 2019.

Winter, Kari J. *Subjects of Slavery, Agents of Change: Women and Power in Gothic Novels and Slave Narratives, 1790–1865*. U Georgia P, 1992.

Woods, Scott. "28 More Picture Books That Aren't about Boycotts, Buses or Basketball (2018)." *Scott Woods Makes Lists*, 7 Feb. 2018, https://scottwoodsmakeslists.wordpress.com/2018/02/07/28-more-black-picture-books-that-arent-about-boycotts-buses-or-basketball-2018/. Accessed 28 Feb. 2018.

Zorn, Eric. "Language Matters: The Shift from 'Slave' to 'Enslaved Person' May Be Difficult, but It's Important." *Chicago Tribune*, 6 Sep. 2019, https://www.chicagotribune.com/columns/eric-zorn/ct-column-slave-enslaved-language-people-first-debate-zorn-20190906-audknctayrarfijimpz6uk7hvy-story.html. Accessed 9 Mar. 2021.

INDEX

Ancrum, K., 56–57, 131n; *The Weight of the Stars*, 56–57, 131n
Archer, Jermaine O., 31

Baccolini, Raffiella, 63
Bailey, K. V., 91, 132n
Ballard, J. G., 27, 36; *High Rise*, 27, 36
Barnes, Brooks, 61
Barnes, Steven, xxviii, 54–55, 57, 59–66, 68, 71–78, 80–82
Barr, Marlene S., 60–61
Basu, Balaka, 10
Beaulieu, Elizabeth Ann, 3, 12–13, 17
Bernstein, Robin, 117–19
#BlackGirlMagic, 121, 128
Black Lives Matter, xv, xviii, 55, 63
Black Panther, ix, xi, 129n
Boster, Dea H., 78, 124
Bradford, Clare, 44
Broad, Katherine R., 10
Bruce, Dickson D., Jr., xiii, xxii, xxvii
Budick, Emily Miller, 90
Butler, Octavia E., xv, xix, 15–16, 59, 61–79, 81, 105, 111–13; "The Evening and the Morning and the Night," 71–72; *Kindred*, xv, xix, 15–16, 67, 91, 111–13; *Parable of the Sower*, 59, 63–79, 81, 91; Parables series, xxviii, 54, 59

Carby, Hazel, 117, 132n
CBC (*Canadian Broadcasting Corporation*), xi

Clark, P. Djèlí, xxviii–xxix, 94, 103, 106–8, 113–20; *The Black God's Drums*, xxviii–xxix, 94, 103–8, 113–20, 122
Collins, Suzanne, 10–12, 15, 18, 70, 85; *The Hunger Games*, 10–12, 15, 18, 70, 85; *The Hunger Games* (film), 85
Connolly, Paula T., 29–31, 34, 37–38, 109
Couzelis, Mary J., 17, 85–86
Crenshaw, Kimberlé, 74–75

Day, Sara, 4–5
Deonn, Tracy, xviii; *Bloodmarked*, 122n; *Legendborn*, xviii, 122n
Dery, Mark, xvi, 64, 84
Devil's Wake (novel), 57, 59–66, 68, 71–78, 80–82. *See also* Barnes, Steven; Due, Tananarive
Devil's Wake series, xxviii, 54–55. *See also* Barnes, Steven; Due, Tananarive
Dickens, Charles, 94; Fagin, 94, 114; *Oliver Twist*, 114
Dixon, Melvin, 62
Doc McStuffins, 61
Doll, Jen, 86
Domino Falls (novel), 82. *See also* Barnes, Steven; Due, Tananarive
Douglass, Frederick, xx–xxviii, 13, 20, 35, 65–68, 79, 115; *The Narrative of the Life of Frederick Douglass, An American Slave*, xx–xxviii, 13, 20, 35, 65–68

Driscoll, Catherine, 64–65
Du Bois, W. E. B., 58, 83, 105–6, 131n; "The Comet," 105
Dubey, Madhu, 17
Due, Tananarive, xxviii, 54–55, 57, 59–66, 68, 71–78, 80–82
Dumezweni, Nomi, 85–86
Durgan, Jessica, 93

Elphick, Keith, 5–6, 10, 14, 16, 18, 20, 26
Equiano, Olaudah, ix, xvii; *The Interesting Narrative of the Life of Olaudah Equiano, or Gustavus Vassa, the African. Written by Himself*, ix
Eyerman, Ron, 104

family, 12–13, 22, 39–40, 47–53, 72–78, 91, 96, 100–101, 112, 131n
Flagel, Nadine, 111–12
Foster, Frances Scott, 108–10, 112, 114, 116, 122
Fulton, DoVeanna S., 106

Gates, Henry Louis, Jr., 67
Gibbs, Alan, xxv
Gilbert-Hickey, Meghan, 18
Glasner, Eli, xi
Gomez, Jewelle, xviii; *The Gilda Stories*, xviii
Goyal, Yogita, xv, 130n
Green-Barteet, Miranda, 4–5

Harlem Renaissance, 58, 80, 83, 105, 125
Harris, Kamala, 76
Harris, Trudier, 38–41, 43–44, 98–99
Harris-Perry, Melissa V., 75
Harry Potter and the Cursed Child (play), 85
Hartley, A. J., xvi–xvii, 85–102, 131n; "Chains," 87; *Firebrand*, 97; *The Guardian*, 97; "A Head for Heights," 87, 92; *Steeplejack*, xvi–xvii, 85–102; Steeplejack series, 86; "Writing POC While White," 86–87
Hill Collins, Patricia, xii–xiv
Hintz, Carrie, 10
Hollywood Diversity Report, ix, 129n
hooks, bell, 60, 93
Hopkinson, Nalo, ix; *Brown Girl in the Ring*, ix
Hurston, Zora Neale, 60, 80, 105–6; *Tell My Horse*, 80; *Their Eyes Were Watching God*, 105–6

Ireland, Justina, xxiii–xxix, 80, 103–4, 106–8, 120–28; *Deathless Divide*, 91, 106–8, 123, 125–28; *Dread Nation*, 103, 105–8, 120–28; Dread Nation series, xxiii–xxix, 80

Jacobs, Harriet, xxiii, xxvii–xxviii, 67, 115–17; *Incidents in the Life of a Slave Girl*, xxiii, 115–17
Jones, Gayl, 111; *Corregidora*, 111

Kawin, Bruce, 64–65, 79–80, 82
Keckley, Elizabeth, 116; *Behind the Scenes. By Elizabeth Keckley, Formerly a Slave, but More Recently Modiste, and Friend to Mrs. Abraham Lincoln. Or, Thirty Years a Slave, and Four Years in the White House*, 116
Kilgore, De Witt Douglas, 64, 84
King, Debra Walker, 23–24
Koss, Melanie D., 8–9
Kritzer, Naomi, 55; *Catfishing on CatNet*, 55

Lacks, Henrietta, 76
Larsen, Nella, 125; *Passing*, 125
Lavender, Isiah, xvii

INDEX

Lawrence, Jennifer, 85
Lemon, Don, 96
Leonard, Elizabeth Anne, 4, 85
Levitas, Ruth, 5
Lorde, Audre, 122–23
Lundquist, Lynne, 99

MacCann, Donnarae, xxi
Mafe, Diana Adesola, 121, 124, 127, 132n
Manganelli, Kimberly Snyder, 125–26
Mann, Catherine, 42–43
Marotta, Melanie A., 73
McArthur, Sherell A., 74
McConnell, Kelsey, xix
McDuffe, Kristi, 50–51
Meeusen, Meghann, 104
Mendlesohn, Farah, 8–9, 41–42, 45, 48–52
#MeToo Movement, 101
Montz, Amy, 4–5
Morrison, Toni, x, xv, 44, 89–90, 103, 105, 129n; *Beloved*, xv, 44, 89–91, 103, 125; *The Bluest Eye*, x
Moylan, Tom, 63–64, 70

neo-Victorian genre, 87, 91, 93, 114
Newman, Judie, xvii

Okorafor, Nnedi, xxviii, 27–53; *Binti*, xxviii, 27–28, 48–53; *Binti: Home*, 52; *The Book of Phoenix*, xxviii, 27–48, 49, 52, 130n; "Hello, Moto," 32–33; *Who Fears Death*, 27
Olney, James, 34–35, 67–68
overseer, 94

Porter, Rick, xix
Prince, Mary, ix, xvii; *The History of Mary Prince, A West Indian Slave. Written by Herself*, ix
Pulliam, June, 10–12, 15

Ratcliffe, Rebecca, 85–86
Reed, Ishmael, 103; *Flight to Canada*, 103
Robledo community, 59, 69–71, 77, 79. *See also* Butler, Octavia E.
Romero, George A., 80
Rowe, Karen E., 37
Rowling, J. K., 85, 131n
Rushdy, Ashraf, 3, 17, 89–90

Sandler, Karen, x, 4, 16–26; *Tankborn*, x, 4, 16–26
Santamaria, Xiomara, xiii–xiv
Sargent, Lyman Tower, 62, 73
Sawyer, Andy, 91, 132n
Science Fiction Research Association, 48
Scott, Lynn Orilla, 112–13
shambler(s), 122–23, 127
Shelley, Mary, 35–36, 121; *Frankenstein*, 35–36, 121
Sims, David, x–xi
Sinanan, Kerry, xii–xxiv
Smith, Katharine Capshaw, 83
Smith, Sherri L., x, 3–17, 22, 25–26, 28–59; *Orleans*, x, 3–17, 22, 25–26, 28–59, 130n
Smith, Valerie, 104–5
speciMEN, 27, 32, 36, 38–41, 44–46. *See also* Okorafor, Nnedi
Star Trek (television series), 121; Uhura, 121
Stepto, Robert B., 5, 7, 28–29, 31–32, 35
Sullivan, C. W., 66

Thomson, Rosemarie Garland, 6–8, 46
trauma, xii, xxv–xxvi, 55, 58, 68–69, 77–78, 82, 85, 88, 90–91, 95, 100, 103–4, 107, 110, 113, 122, 128
Trites, Roberta Seelinger, 11–12, 22, 26, 46–48, 50, 58, 94–95, 97, 100–101
Tuskegee Study of Untreated Syphilis in the Negro Male, 76, 130n

Ulanowicz, Anastasia, 88–91, 95, 131n

Varsam, Maria, 63

Waldman, Katy, xxvi
Watson, Steven, 125
Westfahl, Gary, 99

Williams, Imogen Russell, 114
Winter, Kari J., xxi–xxii, xxv
Woods, Scott, 58, 60–61

zombie(s), 64–65, 72, 76–77, 79–82, 91, 104, 106. *See also* shambler(s)
Zorn, Eric, xxvi

ABOUT THE AUTHOR

Melanie A. Marotta is a lecturer in the Department of English and Language Arts at Morgan State University (Baltimore, Maryland). Marotta's research focuses on American literature (in particular African American), young adult literature, the American West, science fiction, and ecocriticism. She coedited *Critical Pedagogy: Diversity, Inclusion, and the Visual in Higher Education* (Routledge, 2021) with Susan Flynn, which is included in Routledge's series Race and Ethnicity in Education. Her collection, *Women's Space: Essays on Female Characters in the 21st Century Science Fiction Western*, was published in 2019 as part of the Critical Explorations in Science Fiction and Fantasy Series. She is currently working on a second monograph about young adult literature. Marotta is originally from Ontario, Canada.

www.ingramcontent.com/pod-product-compliance
Lightning Source LLC
Chambersburg PA
CBHW030625230426
43661CB00053B/2145